THE HEALTHY
Air Fryer
COOKBOOK

Fried Green Tomatoes, p. 135

THE HEALTHY
Air Fryer
COOKBOOK

*Truly Healthy Fried Food Recipes with
Low Salt, Low Fat, and Zero Guilt*

LINDA LARSEN

FALL RIVER PRESS

New York

To my dear husband, Doug;
my beautiful nieces, Maddie and Grace;
and my wonderful nephew, Michael.
They are a joy and a delight!

FALL RIVER PRESS

New York

An Imprint of Sterling Publishing Co., Inc.
1166 Avenue of the Americas
New York, NY 10036

ISBN 978-1-4351-6733-9

For information about custom editions, special sales, and premium and corporate purchases, please contact
Sterling Special Sales at 800-805-5489 or specialsales@sterlingpublishing.com.

Manufactured in China

2 4 6 8 10 9 7 5 3 1

sterlingpublishing.com

CONTENTS

INTRODUCTION

The air fryer—the first truly new appliance introduced to home cooks in decades—is a wonderful piece of kitchen equipment! It is. It literally fries foods using hot dry air—not oil—that circulates around each piece, sealing in the flavor and creating a crust with a fabulous crunch. Yes, crunch.

With this appliance you can re-create and enjoy those deep-fried foods you may have given up—donuts, French fries, fried chicken—and take this concept a step further. If you want to cook foods that are not just better for you than deep-fried foods, but also actually healthy, good-for-you foods in and of themselves, this book can help you do just that.

I have always loved fried foods. Growing up, for our birthday dinners, we were allowed to choose our favorite meal. Mine was grilled steak served with home-made French fries that were (gulp) fried in an entire can of solid shortening. That is not a meal I choose today, but, using the air fryer, I can have similar foods that taste even better and that are *actually good for me*!

When I first ventured into cooking healthy foods in the air fryer, I was committed to learning to cook food with less fat and better nutrition. Like you, I'm sure, I also wanted it to taste good and be quick and easy. I love to try new appliances, and this sounded simple. However, I admit I was slightly skeptical at first—would shrimp toast made with whole-wheat-breaded veggies taste good? Could I possibly create a donut hole that was healthy yet still yummy? Yes—the answer is yes. And the most surprising thing of all? Foods cooked with just hot air can be as crisp and flavorful as those cooked in fat. What's not to love?

In this book, you'll find 109 recipes that don't just claim to be healthy, but that are truly healthy—heart healthy—along with the nutritional information to back up that claim. You'll also find tips for using your air fryer, information on how recipes were selected for inclusion in this book, and even more ways to reduce fat and salt and still increase flavor in your favorite foods. Let's get started!

Purple Potato Chips with Chipotle Sauce and Rosemary, p. 58

One

LIGHT AS AIR

The Healthy Way to Fry

In 2008, a company in England invented the air fryer as an alternative to deep fat fryers. An air fryer is a stand-alone appliance that uses a fan to blow hot air on and around your food, cooking it rapidly, while a vent removes moisture and keeps the temperature inside the appliance constant.

To compare:

- **Hot oil** conducts heat very well and cooks food quickly. When you put food into a deep-fat fryer, the water on the food's surface instantly evaporates. Water from inside the food is released, which rapidly moves the oil around, causing the bubbling action of the oil. The food's interior is cooked as the heat moves through the food. The crust starts to brown due to a chemical reaction called the Maillard reaction, in which sugars and proteins on the crust break down and recombine to form compounds that look brown and taste great.

- **Hot air** cooks food more slowly because it does not conduct heat as well as oil or water. To understand the difference, think of how you can put your hand into a 350°F oven for a few seconds, but you cannot put it into boiling water (212°F). To mimic deep-frying, but without all the unhealthy oil, an air fryer uses a fan to push the air around the food to dramatically speed the cooking process. So, just as in a deep-fat fryer, in an air fryer the surface of the food dehydrates, water is released, and the interior cooks in a few minutes. Foods cooked in an air fryer cook 25 percent faster than foods cooked in a conventional oven.

And because little or no oil is used, cooking with an air fryer is a much more versatile way to cook food than cooking with a deep fryer. You can bake, roast, grill, stir-fry, and even steam foods in an air fryer. So instead of just cooking alternatives to fried foods, use this appliance to make foods without those hundreds of added fat calories; it actually will help improve your health and well-being.

While other air fryer cookbooks offer recipes that are certainly healthier than their deep-fried counterparts, this book is the *only one* that offers truly healthy recipes. If you look at the nutrition content of all other air fryer cookbooks, you will see that the recipes are still very high in fat, sodium, and sugars. I developed the recipes in this book to be as low in fat, sodium, and sugars as possible, and high in vitamins and fiber.

AIR-FRYING: STEP BY STEP

You can think of an air fryer as a miniature convection oven. Inside the air fryer, a heater underneath the food heats the air. A slotted pan over the heater lets the superheated air move quickly around the food. A fan keeps the air circulating, and a vent pulls moisture and cooler air out of the appliance so the temperature inside stays high and constant.

Just as in deep-frying, a crust immediately forms on the food in the air fryer. This helps seal in moisture so the interior of the food can cook. The starches inside the food gelatinize, the proteins denature, and the fiber softens as the outside browns—all fancy terms meaning the food cooks as it heats.

Most recipes for air fryers are very similar to recipes cooked in ovens or deep-fried in oil. But there are some essential differences.

- **Batter:** Hot oil instantly solidifies a batter. But in an air fryer, the liquid runs off in the few seconds in takes for the air to heat it. Wet foods will not work in an air fryer.

- **Shape:** Cut foods into similarly sized pieces so everything cooks evenly in your air fryer.
- **Coatings:** Foods coated with bread crumbs, ground nuts, or grated cheeses should be moist enough to ensure those small particles stay on the food and do not drop off into the air fryer and burn.

Once the food is prepared according to the recipe, the air fryer is usually preheated following the instructions that came with your appliance. The food is placed in a basket and inserted into the air fryer before you start timing. In just a few minutes, out comes perfectly cooked, hot, crisp food that is ready to eat.

Good Health Begins with Your Heart

Heart disease is the number one killer in the United States. A diet high in fat and sodium and low in nutrients and fiber can contribute to this epidemic. Changing how we cook the foods we enjoy can play an important role in reducing our risk of developing heart disease.

WHAT AILS US

You've heard the saying "If Momma isn't happy, nobody's happy." For our purposes, let's amend that to "If your heart isn't happy, your body isn't happy." Many ailments that Americans struggle with have a direct impact on heart health. Obesity, high blood pressure, and inflammation can all contribute to heart disease.

The foods we choose to eat directly affect our health. Consuming too much sodium can increase the risk for developing high blood pressure. Eating too much of the wrong types of fat can contribute to obesity. And chronic low-grade inflammation, which is the body's way of responding to foreign invaders such as viruses, can lead to plaque development that clogs your arteries. These ailments can also increase your risk of stroke, diabetes, and even cancer. By focusing on keeping your heart healthy, you automatically decrease your risk of developing other debilitating diseases.

EATING HEART HEALTHY

There are many definitions of the word *healthy* as it pertains to food and your diet, depending on your health concerns and dietary needs. Some people reduce their carbohydrate intake. Others eat only organic foods. Some eliminate entire categories of foods, such as dairy, grains, or legumes.

In this book, we abide by the American Heart Association's (AHA) definition of nourishing, healthy food: *low in fat, high in nutrients and fiber, and low in sodium.* While the AHA no longer recommends a low-fat diet, it does say that Americans should replace saturated fats and trans fats with healthier fats such as monounsaturated and polyunsaturated fats. Most adults should consume about 13 grams of saturated fat a day, which, on a 2,000-calorie-a-day-diet, is 5 to 6 percent of calories from saturated fat. And the AHA recommends the acceptable macronutrient distribution range, issued by the Health and Medicine Division, part of the National Academies of Sciences, Engineering, and Medicine, in 2002. This recommended range, for adults, is 20 to 35 percent of calories from fat.

One tool in the AHA's recommendations is DASH—Dietary Approaches to Stop Hypertension. Hypertension, or high blood pressure, is known as the "silent killer" because usually there are no symptoms. Many Americans don't even know they have it. Thus, the AHA recommends consuming no more than 2,300 milligrams of sodium per day, and preferably 1,500 milligrams per day or fewer. To put that in perspective, one-quarter teaspoon of salt contains 575 milligrams of sodium.

Sugars are another concern. Eating a lot of sugar can increase your risk for heart disease and contributes to inflammation in the body. There are three kinds of sugar:

1 **Glucose:** the main building block of carbohydrates
2 **Fructose:** the sugar found in fruits
3 **Sucrose:** granulated sugar

Most recipes use two kinds of sugar:

1 Naturally occurring sugars (fructose) from fruits and some vegetables
2 Added sugars

Most added sugars in American diets are in soft drinks, candy, cakes, cookies, pies, and some dairy products such as sweetened yogurt. Those sugars have no nutritional value other than calories. Added sugars include brown sugar, white sugar, honey, molasses, and corn syrup; those products have lots of sucrose.

The AHA recommends that men limit their intake of added sugars to 36 grams (9 teaspoons) per day; women should limit their intake to 24 grams (6 teaspoons) per day.

Naturally occurring sugars, such as fructose, are not as bad for you as added sugars. Those natural sugars come packaged with lots of vitamins A and C and fiber. And the fiber helps slow your body's processing of sugar, which decreases the rate at which your blood sugar rises. That may help prevent the development of diabetes.

The AHA also recommends that Americans reduce the number of calories they eat. Most people should eat about 2,000 calories a day, depending on age, sex, and level of physical activity. You should eat a variety of foods, with an emphasis on fruits and vegetables, whole grains, lean meats, poultry, fish, low-fat dairy products, nuts, legumes, and vegetable oils. Choose foods that are high in fiber, avoid trans fats (more on this fat later) and saturated fat, and cut back on sugar consumption.

On this diet, every day, you should eat:

- **Dairy (low fat):** two or three servings
- **Fats and oils:** two or three servings
- **Fruit:** four or five servings
- **Vegetables:** four or five servings
- **Meat, poultry, and fish:** six or fewer servings
- **Grains:** about six servings

And, if you are serious about improving your health, it's worth your while to make sure you understand exactly what a "serving" is (see Resources, page 157). Most Americans think a serving is much larger than it actually is. For example:

- **Bread**: One serving is one (1-ounce) slice.
- **Fruit:** One serving is one piece.
- **Ice cream:** One serving (sadly) is just ½ cup.
- **Meat:** One 3-ounce serving is about the size of a deck of cards.

All recipes included in this book have, per serving:

- No more than 35 percent of calories from fat
- No more than 140 milligrams of sodium per serving
- Only 1 to 2 grams of saturated fat, in most cases
- No more than 22 grams of sugar (most have much less)
- No trans fat
- Healthy amounts of vitamins and fiber, when possible

TRIM THE FAT—AND SALT

It's not difficult to cut down on fat and salt in your favorite foods; it just takes a little knowledge and effort.

Did you know that most sodium you consume is in packaged and processed foods? Reduce sodium by:

- reading the labels and buying low-sodium versions of your favorite foods.
- choosing whole foods, such as fresh tomatoes and chicken breasts, instead of a frozen chicken dinner.
- reducing or eliminating salt added to recipes you cook. Sprinkle a tiny bit of salt on your food right before you eat it—the flavor will be more apparent, and you will be more satisfied.

To cut fat from your diet, trim visible fat off meat, remove the skin from poultry before cooking it, and choose lower-fat products, such as turkey sausage instead of pork sausage. And, again, read labels when buying processed foods and choose low-fat options.

OTHER DIETS AND HEART HEALTH

The main dietary approaches to good heart health include the DASH diet, on which this book was based; plant-based diets such as vegetarian and vegan; and the Mediterranean diet, which emphasizes whole foods, fresh produce, and olive oil. All these diets are compatible with the recipes in this book.

You Are What You Eat

Plainly put, your body reflects what you put into it. If you eat a lot of foods high in fat, your body may contain more fat. If you eat a lot of sugar, your blood sugar levels may rise. And if you consume many foods high in sodium, your blood pressure may increase. Think of food as the building blocks for your body. It's much easier to say no to those deep-fried French fries if you know that the fat will travel to your heart where, it will, ultimately, do damage.

CHOOSE WISELY

In the supermarket, not all ingredients are created equal. The nutritional difference between a cream puff and a tomato is obvious, but there's also a big difference in nutrition between a fresh red bell pepper and a wrinkled tomato. Withered produce not only looks unappealing, but it also has fewer nutrients than produce that is plump and heavy, and it may harbor more bacteria. Look carefully at everything you pick up before you put it in your cart.

Quick Picks

When you shop, look for certain things to get the most nutrition for your money:

1. In the meat department, look for plump meats, poultry, and seafood with little fat and a fresh, clean aroma.
2. Always check dates on packaged foods for the best quality. If you buy packaged greens, for instance, select the package with the date furthest in the future.
3. Read labels. Choose foods that adhere to the AHA guidelines—low in fat, high in nutrients and fiber, and low in sodium.
4. In the produce aisle, choose heavy fruits and vegetables with smooth skin and no blemishes, cuts, soft spots, or bruises. The color should be deep and even.
5. Ripe fruits should give slightly when gently pressed with your fingers, but they should not be overly soft. They should be heavy for their size, too.

VERY VALUABLE VEGGIES

This book's recipes use basic vegetables that are available at any grocery store and are key to a healthy diet. These foods are high in nutrients and have very little sodium and fat.

SEASONAL EATING

You may notice the inclusion of "season available" in the table that follows on page 16. Seasonal eating is also important to good health. Fruits and vegetables have a higher vitamin content when you eat them in season; they are fresher because they haven't been shipped long distances to get to your plate, so their taste and nutrients haven't decreased. These foods lose nutrients as soon as they are harvested.

In the summer, of course, fresh produce is readily available everywhere. But in the fall and winter, many brightly colored fruits and veggies you see in the store have been shipped from miles away.

VEGGIE	HOW TO PURCHASE	MAIN NUTRIENTS	NUTRIENT BENEFITS	SEASON AVAILABLE
Asparagus	Buy asparagus that is firm and unbruised with tips that are tightly closed.	Contains vitamins C and K and fiber	High in saponins, which are anti-inflammatory	Spring
Bell peppers	Look for brightly colored peppers that are firm with smooth skin.	Good source of vitamins A and C and carotenoids that give the vegetable its amazing color	Carotenoids act as antioxidants with strong cancer-fighting properties.	All
Broccoli	Choose broccoli heads that are heavy, with tightly closed florets that are a deep green color.	Good source of vitamins A and D	Contains many compounds that help prevent cancer, such as indoles and sulforaphane	All
Carrots	Choose carrots that are firm, brightly colored, smooth, and not wrinkled.	High in vitamins A and C, potassium, and fiber	Good source of fiber	All
Garlic	Look for firm heads with no soft spots.	Good source of vitamins C and B and copper	Contains allicin, which helps lower cholesterol	All
Leafy greens	Should be brightly colored with no bruises or broken leaves	Lots of magnesium and iron; low in carbs	High in fiber and vitamin C, which help protect heart health	All
Mushrooms	Mushrooms should be firm and evenly colored, with no bruises or dark spots. Look for tightly closed caps.	Good source of vitamins B and D and minerals	Contains lots of vitamin D, which helps protect bone health	All
Onions	Buy firm, heavy onions with tightly attached skin.	Polyphenols and flavonoids; also high in biotin, manganese, vitamin B_6, and potassium	Contains antioxidants such as quercetin that help prevent inflammation	All
Sweet potatoes	Look for heavy, firm sweet potatoes with no soft spots or bruises.	Good source of vitamins A and B and manganese	Contains lots of fiber that helps reduce blood sugar levels	Fall Winter
Tomatoes	Buy firm, heavy tomatoes with smooth skin and no soft spots or bruises.	Great source of vitamins A and C and lycopene	Antioxidant that can help lower cholesterol levels	Summer Fall

To get the most nutrients from your foods no matter the season, consider these guidelines:

- **In summer:** Go crazy cooking with just about every fruit and veggie on the shelf. This is peak season for fresh berries, corn, tomatoes, and other soft fruits and vegetables.
- **In fall**: Rely on leafy greens, sweet potatoes, pears, squash, cauliflower, and mushrooms.
- **In winter:** Eat Brussels sprouts, oranges, apples, and sweet potatoes.
- **In spring:** Select asparagus, artichokes, peas, spinach, and strawberries.

WHEN TO GO ORGANIC

And here's an interesting question: Should you buy organic foods? Organic foods are those that are grown without artificial fertilizers, pesticides, and herbicides. Unfortunately, the produce in most American grocery stores is grown using conventional methods, and pesticide residue has been measured on many of these foods.

Some consumer advocates have created a list of the "cleanest" and "dirtiest" fruits and vegetables at the supermarket (see Appendix B, page 155). If you are concerned about pesticide residues on your foods, buy these five foods organically grown, if you can:

1 Apples
2 Peaches
3 Celery
4 Tomatoes
5 Bell peppers

Healthy Oils

Some recipes in this book use a tiny bit of oil to help foods brown and crisp. Any oil will work, but some are better than others. Because the temperature inside the air fryer can be set up to 400ºF, only use oils that have high *smoke points*. That is the temperature at which the oil begins to break down and release smoke.

The oils with the highest smoke points include:

1 Corn
2 Extra-light olive
3 Grapeseed
4 Peanut
5 Safflower

All these oils are unsaturated, which means they fit into the American Heart Association's guidelines for a healthy diet. And not one of them contains any trans fat, a type of artificial fat that is particularly bad for your heart.

One of the healthiest fats for cooking is olive oil, because it can increase good cholesterol and reduce bad cholesterol in your blood. Olive oil may also help you reduce the risk of developing type 2 diabetes and stroke.

Air Fryer Safety, Troubleshooting, and Care

The air fryer is a very safe appliance because the cooking process takes place inside a sealed container. But, as safe as this appliance is, you must still handle it with care. Before you begin any cooking, read the instruction manual that came with your specific air fryer for basic safety tips and instructions on use.

SAFETY

Always place the air fryer on a stable, heat-proof surface. Don't use an extension cord to plug it in. While the fryer is operating, steam that can burn comes out of the vents—stay away from these vents while the fryer is operating. Some additional tips to stay safe:

- Be careful when removing the basket from the air fryer; it is very hot.
- Do not tip food out of the fryer, because the pan may contain hot oil or liquid. Tipping it may splash that liquid onto your hands.
- Never press the button that holds the basket and pan together when you remove them from the air fryer.

Safety also includes food safety. Always cook ground meats to an internal temperature of 160ºF, pork to 145ºF, chicken to 165ºF, and fish to 140ºF. Check these temperatures with a meat thermometer.

TROUBLESHOOTING

All air fryers are a bit different, so always read the instruction manual that came with your machine. Each brand may suggest different cooking times and temperatures for different types of cooking and foods.

My top tips for troubleshooting:

- Sometimes you must manipulate the food while it cooks. Shake the basket or turn larger foods, such as steaks or chicken, to make sure they cook evenly.

- Not crisp? If the food does not crisp, it may have been too wet. Pat foods dry before putting them into the basket. Coating some foods, such as marinated meat, with cornstarch or flour can also help them crisp up.
- White smoke that appears as the food cooks means that foods are too wet; some of that smoke is probably steam or from tiny particles of food stuck to the inside of the fryer.
- Black smoke is a sign of a problem. If you see black smoke, immediately turn off the machine, unplug it, let it cool, and take it to an appliance repairman.

CLEANING AND CARING

The manual that came with your air fryer will discuss how to clean and care for it. To clean most fryers, unplug and let the machine cool. Remove the basket and pan and wash them with soap and water using a plastic scrubbing brush—*never use steel wool*. If food is stuck onto these pieces, soak them in warm water for about 10 minutes before washing with soap and water. Some parts of your air fryer may be dishwasher safe; check the manual before cleaning this way.

After each cooking session, check inside the appliance for stray crumbs or bits of food and remove them. Wipe the outside and inside of the appliance with a damp paper towel or sponge. Finally, check the bottom of the machine. If there is any grease or oil there, soak it up with paper towels and wipe it clean with a cloth.

About the Recipes

The 109 recipes in this book were chosen for their nutrient density, adherence to AHA guidelines, ease of preparation, and quick cooking. With very few exceptions, you'll be ready to eat in 30 minutes or less, start to finish. And almost every recipe requires no more than eight everyday ingredients to prepare (not including cooking spray to prepare the pan, a small amount of water needed for cooking, or optional accompaniments). All recipes include nutritional information, and each is labeled with a few defining words to help you choose, including:

- Family Favorite
- Fast (ready to eat in 15 minutes or less, start to finish)
- Gluten Free
- No Sodium (fewer than 5 grams of sodium per serving)
- Vegan (no animal products)
- Vegetarian (may include dairy, eggs, or honey)
- Very Low Sodium (recipes with less than 35 grams of sodium per serving)

Some recipes transform foods traditionally deep-fat fried into healthier options, while other foods are baked, grilled, roasted, or stir-fried to demonstrate how versatile your air fryer is.

Each recipe has a set upper limit on the amount of fat and sodium—no more than 35 percent of calories from fat and no more than 140 milligrams of sodium per serving—and includes foods that provide essential nutrients.

You can see how healthy each recipe is using the nutritional information provided, which includes:

- Calories per serving
- Fat (percentage of calories from fat)
- Saturated fat
- Protein
- Carbohydrate
- Sodium, in milligrams
- Fiber
- Sugar
- DV vitamins ("DV " is the daily value of nutrients—vitamins and minerals—the typical healthy adult needs to consume every day based on a 2,000-calorie diet)

And to feel really good about these foods, 30 recipes (about one-third of the total) include a comparison called "Aren't You Glad You Didn't Deep-Fry?," which tells you the main difference between your healthier air-fried version and the traditional deep-fried preparation. Proof again, with so many recipes that are not just remade deep-fried alternatives, of how healthy this way of cooking can be.

Let's cook!

Carrot and Cinnamon Muffins, p. 30

BREAKFAST

Veggie Frittata

PREP 10 minutes / **COOK** 8 to 12 minutes / **SERVES** 4

350°F

Gluten-Free, Vegetarian

½ cup chopped
red bell pepper

⅓ cup minced onion

⅓ cup grated carrot

1 teaspoon olive oil

6 egg whites

1 egg

⅓ cup 2 percent milk

1 tablespoon grated
Parmesan cheese

A frittata is like an omelet, only sturdier. Frittatas are so easy to make in the air fryer. This egg recipe is usually baked until it is puffy and golden. Cook the vegetables first so they are tender, add the egg and milk mixture, and bake until done.

1 In a 6-by-2-inch pan, stir together the red bell pepper, onion, carrot, and olive oil. Put the pan into the air fryer. Cook for 4 to 6 minutes, shaking the basket once, until the vegetables are tender.

2 Meanwhile, in a medium bowl, beat the egg whites, egg, and milk until combined.

3 Pour the egg mixture over the vegetables in the pan. Sprinkle with the Parmesan cheese. Return the pan to the air fryer.

4 Bake for 4 to 6 minutes more, or until the frittata is puffy and set.

5 Cut into 4 wedges and serve.

NUTRITION NOTE The percentage of calories from fat in this recipe is relatively high because the overall calories are so low. This is still a very low-fat recipe.

PER SERVING Calories: 77; Fat: 3g (35% calories from fat); Saturated Fat: 1g; Protein: 8g; Carbohydrates: 5g; Sodium: 116mg; Fiber: 1g; Sugar: 3g; 14% DV vitamin A; 62% DV vitamin C

Salmon and Brown Rice Frittata

PREP 15 minutes / **COOK** 15 minutes / **SERVES** 4

320°F

Gluten-Free

Olive oil, for greasing the pan

1 egg

4 egg whites

½ teaspoon dried thyme

½ cup cooked brown rice

½ cup cooked, flaked salmon (about 3 ounces)

½ cup fresh baby spinach (see Tip)

¼ cup chopped red bell pepper

1 tablespoon grated Parmesan cheese

Brown rice is much better for you than white rice because it contains the outer layer known as the bran, which makes it a whole grain. This layer contains fiber and nutrients such as manganese. And salmon is one of the best protein choices you can make; it is a lean protein and contains omega-3 fatty acids that help protect your heart. This frittata is a great choice for starting a busy morning off right.

1 Rub a 6-by-2-inch pan with a bit of olive oil and set aside.

2 In a small bowl, beat the egg, egg whites, and thyme until well mixed.

3 In the prepared pan, stir together the brown rice, salmon, spinach, and red bell pepper.

4 Pour the egg mixture over the rice mixture and sprinkle with the Parmesan cheese.

5 Bake for about 15 minutes, or until the frittata is puffed and golden brown. Serve.

SUBSTITUTION TIP Use other greens instead of baby spinach if you prefer. Try chopped kale for extra fiber and nutrition; microgreens, which are seedlings that pack a nutritional punch; or watercress or arugula for a peppery flavor.

PER SERVING Calories: 97; Fat: 3g (27% calories from fat); Saturated Fat: 1; Protein: 11g; Carbohydrates: 7g; Sodium: 115mg; Fiber: 1g; Sugar: 1g; 14% DV vitamin A; 31% DV vitamin C

Avocado and Egg Burrito

PREP 10 minutes / **COOK** 3 to 5 minutes / **SERVES** 4

390°F

Family Favorite, Fast, Vegetarian

2 hardboiled egg whites, chopped

1 hardboiled egg, chopped

1 avocado, peeled, pitted, and chopped

1 red bell pepper, chopped

3 tablespoons low-sodium salsa, plus additional for serving (optional)

1 (1.2-ounce) slice low-sodium, low-fat American cheese, torn into pieces

4 low-sodium whole-wheat flour tortillas (see Tip)

AREN'T YOU GLAD YOU DIDN'T DEEP-FRY

Your total calories have been reduced by more than half.

Burritos are very popular for breakfast because you can eat them on the run—and they are versatile and delicious. However, most can also be loaded with fat and sodium. This lighter version bursts with vegetables and a couple of hardboiled eggs.

1 In a medium bowl, thoroughly mix the egg whites, egg, avocado, red bell pepper, salsa, and cheese.

2 Place the tortillas on a work surface and evenly divide the filling among them. Fold in the edges and roll up. Secure the burritos with toothpicks if necessary.

3 Put the burritos in the air fryer basket. Air-fry for 3 to 5 minutes, or until the burritos are light golden brown and crisp. Serve with more salsa (if using).

COOKING TIP You may want to soften the tortillas before you roll them. To do this, wrap the tortillas in aluminum foil and air-fry them for 1 to 2 minutes.

PER SERVING Calories: 204; Fat: 8g (35% calories from fat); Saturated Fat: 2g; Protein: 9g; Carbohydrates: 27g; Sodium: 109mg; Fiber: 3g; Sugar: 1g; 11% DV vitamin A; 33% DV vitamin C

Asparagus and Bell Pepper Strata

PREP 10 minutes / **COOK** 14 to 20 minutes / **SERVES** 4

330°F

Vegetarian

8 large asparagus spears, trimmed and cut into 2-inch pieces

⅓ cup shredded carrot (see Tip)

½ cup chopped red bell pepper

2 slices low-sodium whole-wheat bread, cut into ½-inch cubes

3 egg whites

1 egg

3 tablespoons 1 percent milk

½ teaspoon dried thyme

A strata is a mixture of bread, eggs, and cheese that is baked until puffy and light. This version is lighter and healthier because it contains whole-grain bread, adds vegetables, and uses mostly egg whites and low-fat cheese. Bakery bread can contain very high levels of sodium. If you must reduce sodium in your diet, look for low-sodium varieties or bake your own and add very little salt. Serve this warm dish for breakfast with fresh fruit and orange juice.

1 In a 6-by-2-inch pan, combine the asparagus, carrot, red bell pepper, and 1 tablespoon of water. Bake in the air fryer for 3 to 5 minutes, or until crisp-tender. Drain well.

2 Add the bread cubes to the vegetables and gently toss.

3 In a medium bowl, whisk the egg whites, egg, milk, and thyme until frothy.

4 Pour the egg mixture into the pan. Bake for 11 to 15 minutes, or until the strata is slightly puffy and set and the top starts to brown. Serve.

INGREDIENT TIP You can buy shredded carrots at the grocery store, but it's much cheaper to shred your own. Use the largest holes on a box grater. About ½ large carrot equals ⅓ cup shredded.

PER SERVING Calories: 100; Fat: 2g (18% of calories from fat); Saturated Fat: 0g; Protein: 9g; Carbohydrates: 14g; Sodium: 129mg; Fiber: 3g; Sugar: 5g; 50% DV vitamin A; 65% DV vitamin C

Chicken Sausages

PREP 15 minutes / **COOK** 8 to 12 minutes / **MAKES** 8 sausage patties

330°F

Gluten-Free,
Very Low Sodium

1 Granny Smith apple, peeled and finely chopped

⅓ cup minced onion

3 tablespoons ground almonds

2 garlic cloves, minced

1 egg white

2 tablespoons apple juice

⅛ teaspoon freshly ground black pepper

1 pound ground chicken breast

AREN'T YOU GLAD YOU DIDN'T DEEP-FRY

The percentage of calories from fat drops from 78 to 21 percent. That's impressive.

Sausage for breakfast is a great idea, but it is typically loaded with fat and salt. This recipe is different. We start with ground chicken and add onions, garlic, and apple for flavor and nutrition. Unlike fried sausage patties, you can enjoy these guilt-free.

1 In a medium bowl, thoroughly mix the apple, onion, almonds, garlic, egg white, apple juice, and pepper.

2 With your hands, gently work the chicken breast into the apple mixture until combined.

3 Form the mixture into 8 patties. Put the patties into the air fryer basket. You may need to cook them in batches. Air-fry for 8 to 12 minutes, or until the patties reach an internal temperature of 165ºF on a meat thermometer (see Tip). Serve.

COOKING TIP To use a meat thermometer properly on these little sausages, hold the sausages with tongs and insert the thermometer's probe into the side of the patty. Try to hit the middle of each patty. For food safety, always cook ground chicken to 165°F and other ground meats to 160°F.

PER SERVING (1 patty) Calories: 87; Fat: 2g (21% calories from fat); Saturated Fat: 0g; Protein: 14g; Carbohydrates: 5g; Sodium: 27mg; Fiber: 1g; Sugar 4g; 6% DV vitamin C

Pumpkin Donut Holes

PREP 15 minutes / **COOK** 14 minutes / **MAKES** 12 donut holes

360°F

Vegetarian, Very Low Sodium

1 cup whole-wheat pastry flour, plus more as needed

3 tablespoons packed brown sugar

½ teaspoon ground cinnamon

1 teaspoon low-sodium baking powder

⅓ cup canned no-salt-added pumpkin purée (not pumpkin pie filling; see Tip)

3 tablespoons 2 percent milk, plus more as needed

2 tablespoons unsalted butter, melted

1 egg white

Powdered sugar (optional)

AREN'T YOU GLAD YOU DIDN'T DEEP-FRY

You just trimmed your total fat calories by more than half.

Donut holes are a well-loved deep-fried breakfast treat, but they are not at all healthy. Adding puréed pumpkin helps cut the fat and adds a lot of vitamin A and fiber. Coat these little treats in cinnamon sugar or powdered sugar, if you like, before serving.

1 In a medium bowl, mix the pastry flour, brown sugar, cinnamon, and baking powder.

2 In a small bowl, beat the pumpkin, milk, butter, and egg white until combined. Add the pumpkin mixture to the dry ingredients and mix until combined. You may need to add more flour or milk to form a soft dough.

3 Divide the dough into 12 pieces. With floured hands, form each piece into a ball.

4 Cut a piece of parchment paper or aluminum foil to fit inside the air fryer basket but about 1 inch smaller in diameter. Poke holes in the paper or foil and place it in the basket.

5 Put 6 donut holes into the basket, leaving some space around each. Air-fry for 5 to 7 minutes, or until the donut holes reach an internal temperature of 200°F and are firm and light golden brown.

6 Let cool for 5 minutes. Remove from the basket and roll in powdered sugar, if desired. Repeat with the remaining donut holes and serve.

INGREDIENT TIP Don't use pumpkin pie filling in this recipe, as it contains sugar, fat, and emulsifiers that will make the dough too runny.

PER SERVING (2 donut holes) Calories: 142; Fat: 4g (25% calories from fat); Saturated Fat: 3g; Protein: 3g; Carbohydrates: 23g; Sodium: 24mg; Fiber: 3g; Sugar: 7g; 45% DV vitamin A

Carrot and Cinnamon Muffins

PREP 15 minutes / **COOK** 12 to 17 minutes / **MAKES** 8 muffins

320°F

Vegetarian

1½ cups whole-wheat pastry flour

1 teaspoon low-sodium baking powder

⅓ cup brown sugar

½ teaspoon ground cinnamon

1 egg

2 egg whites

⅔ cup almond milk

3 tablespoons safflower oil

½ cup finely shredded carrots

⅓ cup golden raisins, chopped

Did you know that you can add almost any fruit or vegetable to a muffin recipe? Everything from diced pears to shredded zucchini or carrots will add wonderful color, texture, flavor, and nutrition to these little breakfast breads.

1 In a medium bowl, combine the flour, baking powder, brown sugar, and cinnamon, and mix well.

2 In a small bowl, combine the egg, egg whites, almond milk, and oil and beat until combined. Stir the egg mixture into the dry ingredients just until combined. Don't over-beat; some lumps should be in the batter—that's just fine.

3 Stir the shredded carrot and chopped raisins gently into the batter.

4 Double up 16 foil muffin cups to make 8 cups. Put 4 of the cups into the air fryer and fill ¾ full with the batter.

5 Bake for 12 to 17 minutes or until the tops of the muffins spring back when lightly touched with your finger.

6 Repeat with remaining muffin cups and the remaining batter. Cool the muffins on a wire rack for 10 minutes before serving.

SUBSTITUTION TIP Try shredded zucchini or yellow summer squash in place of the carrots in this recipe. You could also substitute some chopped pecans or walnuts for the golden raisins.

PER SERVING (1 muffin) Calories: 201; Fat: 7g (31% calories from fat); Saturated Fat: 1g; Protein: 4g; Carbohydrates: 32g; Sodium: 74mg; Fiber: 4g; Sugar: 14g; 32% DV vitamin A; 1% DV vitamin C

Cran-Bran Muffins

PREP 15 minutes / **COOK** 15 minutes / **MAKES** 8 muffins

320°F

Family Favorite, Vegetarian

1½ cups bran cereal flakes

1 cup plus 2 tablespoons whole-wheat pastry flour

3 tablespoons packed brown sugar

1 teaspoon low-sodium baking powder

1 cup 2 percent milk

3 tablespoons safflower oil or peanut oil

1 egg

½ cup dried cranberries

Bran muffins are a classic healthy breakfast food. Whole-wheat pastry flour adds fiber and nutrition, and dried cranberries provide extra flavor and a punch of color. These muffins are easily made in the air fryer. Enjoy them with a glass of orange juice for a great breakfast.

1 In a medium bowl, mix the cereal, pastry flour, brown sugar, and baking powder.

2 In a small bowl, whisk the milk, oil, and egg until combined.

3 Stir the egg mixture into the dry ingredients until just combined (see Tip).

4 Stir in the cranberries.

5 Double up 16 foil muffin cups to make 8 cups. Put 4 cups into the air fryer and fill each three-fourths full with batter. Bake for about 15 minutes, or until the muffin tops spring back when lightly touched with your finger.

6 Repeat with the remaining muffin cups and batter.

7 Let cool on a wire rack for 10 minutes before serving.

PREPARATION TIP For the best muffins, don't stir the batter very much—only until the dry ingredients disappear into the wet ingredients. There may be some lumps in the batter; that's okay. Your muffins will be tough if the batter is overmixed.

PER SERVING (1 muffin) Calories: 192; Fat: 7g (33% calories from fat); Saturated Fat: 1g; Protein: 4g; Carbohydrates: 30g; Sodium: 75mg; Fiber: 4g; Sugar: 12g; 6% DV vitamin C

Dried Fruit Beignets

PREP 22 minutes / **COOK** 5 to 8 minutes / **MAKES** 16 beignets

330°F

Vegetarian, Very Low Sodium

1 teaspoon active quick-rising dry yeast

⅓ cup buttermilk

3 tablespoons packed brown sugar

1 egg

1½ cups whole-wheat pastry flour

3 tablespoons chopped dried cherries

3 tablespoons chopped golden raisins

2 tablespoons unsalted butter, melted

Powdered sugar, for dusting (optional)

AREN'T YOU GLAD YOU DIDN'T DEEP-FRY

Who needs an extra 548 milligrams of sodium to start the day?

Beignets are a classic New Orleans breakfast treat— but they are not healthy. Using whole-wheat pastry flour, less sugar, and dried fruit, this version is much healthier than the traditional one, but still with that touch of New Orleans fun.

1 In a medium bowl, mix the yeast with 3 tablespoons of water. Let it stand for 5 minutes, or until it bubbles.

2 Stir in the buttermilk, brown sugar, and egg until well mixed.

3 Stir in the pastry flour until combined.

4 With your hands, work the cherries and raisins into the dough. Let the mixture stand for 15 minutes.

5 Pat the dough into an 8-by-8-inch square and cut into 16 pieces. Gently shape each piece into a ball.

6 Drizzle the balls with the melted butter. Place them in a single layer in the air fryer basket so they don't touch. You may have to cook these in batches. Air-fry for 5 to 8 minutes, or until puffy and golden brown.

7 Dust with powdered sugar before serving, if desired.

COOKING TIP You can make these in muffin tins sprayed with nonstick cooking spray containing flour. Place one beignet in each muffin cup and air-fry for the same amount of time.

PER SERVING (1 beignet) Calories: 162; Fat: 4g (22% of calories from fat); Saturated Fat: 2g; Protein: 4g; Carbohydrates: 29g; Sodium: 22mg; Fiber: 3g; Sugar: 10g; 6% DV vitamin A

Three-Berry Dutch Pancake

PREP 10 minutes / COOK 12 to 16 minutes / SERVES 4

330°F

Vegetarian

2 egg whites

1 egg

½ cup whole-wheat pastry flour

½ cup 2 percent milk

1 teaspoon pure vanilla extract

1 tablespoon unsalted butter, melted

1 cup sliced fresh strawberries

½ cup fresh blueberries

½ cup fresh raspberries

A Dutch pancake is not like traditional American pancakes. Here, batter is poured into a cake pan and baked until it puffs. When you take the pan out of the oven, the pancake falls and forms an indentation you can fill with lots of fresh fruit. This is a spectacular breakfast recipe, and it's good for you, too!

1 In a medium bowl, use an eggbeater or hand mixer to quickly mix the egg whites, egg, pastry flour, milk, and vanilla until well combined.

2 Use a pastry brush to grease the bottom of a 6-by-2-inch pan with the melted butter. Immediately pour in the batter and put the basket back in the fryer. Bake for 12 to 16 minutes, or until the pancake is puffed and golden brown.

3 Remove the pan from the air fryer; the pancake will fall. Top with the strawberries, blueberries, and raspberries. Serve immediately.

SUBSTITUTION TIP Use different fruits if you prefer. Sauté some apples in apple juice in the air fryer and use those instead of the berries, or try sliced pears.

PER SERVING Calories: 154; Fat: 5g (29% of calories from fat); Saturated Fat: 3g; Protein: 7g; Carbohydrates: 21g; Sodium: 59mg; Fiber: 4g; Sugar: 6g; 5% DV vitamin A; 50% DV vitamin C

French Toast Sticks with Strawberry Sauce

PREP 6 minutes / **COOK** 10 to 14 minutes / **SERVES** 4

380°F

Family Favorite, Fast, Vegetarian

3 slices low-sodium whole-wheat bread, each cut into 4 strips (see Tip)

1 tablespoon unsalted butter, melted

1 egg

1 egg white

1 tablespoon 2 percent milk

1 tablespoon sugar

1 cup sliced fresh strawberries

1 tablespoon freshly squeezed lemon juice

AREN'T YOU GLAD YOU DIDN'T DEEP-FRY

Your percentage of calories from fat is cut by almost half!

French toast is a quintessential breakfast dish—bread soaked in a custard of eggs and milk and fried in butter until crisp and golden. This treat is usually served with maple syrup or powdered sugar. This healthier version uses whole-wheat bread, and the crisp sticks are cooked in the air fryer. Topping them with a strawberry sauce instead of syrup reduces the sugar and adds nutrition and flavor.

1 Place the bread strips on a plate and drizzle with the melted butter.

2 In a shallow bowl, beat the egg, egg white, milk, and sugar.

3 Dip the bread into the egg mixture and place on a wire rack to let the batter drip off.

4 Air-fry half of the bread strips for 5 to 7 minutes, turning the strips with tongs once during cooking, until golden brown. Repeat with the remaining strips.

5 In a small bowl, mash the strawberries and lemon juice with a fork or potato masher. Serve the strawberry sauce with the French toast sticks.

INGREDIENT TIP Always read bread package labels because some are high in sodium and sugar. If you buy your bread from a bakery, ask if they can provide nutritional information.

PER SERVING Calories: 150; Fat: 5g (30% of calories from fat); Saturated Fat: 2g; Protein: 7g; Carbohydrates: 22g; Sodium: 120mg; Fiber: 3g; Sugar: 8g; 3% DV vitamin A; 43% DV vitamin C

Crustless Veggie Quiche, p. 48

Three

LUNCH

Ratatouille

PREP 14 minutes / **COOK** 12 to 16 minutes / **SERVES** 4

390°F

Vegan, Very Low Sodium

4 Roma tomatoes, seeded and chopped (see Tip)

3 garlic cloves, sliced

1 baby eggplant, peeled and chopped

1 red bell pepper, chopped

1 yellow bell pepper, chopped

1 small onion, chopped

1 teaspoon Italian seasoning

1 teaspoon olive oil

Ratatouille—that delightful mix of roasted vegetables seasoned with herbs—is a vintage French dish. It makes a great lunch served on toasted bread, over pasta, or all by itself. You can also make it ahead and refrigerate it; eat it cold or reheat it in the microwave.

1 In a medium metal bowl, gently combine the tomatoes, garlic, eggplant, red and yellow bell peppers, onion, Italian seasoning, and olive oil.

2 Place the bowl in the air fryer. Roast for 12 to 16 minutes, stirring once, until the vegetables are tender. Serve warm or cold.

PREPARATION TIP To seed the tomatoes, cut each in half. Gently squeeze each tomato half to remove the seeds. Coarsely chop the tomatoes.

PER SERVING Calories: 69; Fat: 2g (26% of calories from fat); Saturated Fat: 0g; Protein: 2g; Carbohydrates: 11g; Sodium: 9mg; Fiber: 2g; Sugar: 3g; 29% DV vitamin A; 243% DV vitamin C

Vegetable Egg Rolls

PREP 15 minutes / **COOK** 7 to 10 minutes / **MAKES** 4 egg rolls

390°F

Vegetarian

½ cup chopped yellow summer squash

⅓ cup grated carrot

½ cup chopped red bell pepper

2 scallions, white and green parts, chopped

1 teaspoon low-sodium soy sauce

4 egg roll wrappers (see Tip)

1 tablespoon cornstarch

1 egg, beaten

AREN'T YOU GLAD YOU DIDN'T DEEP-FRY

Deep-fried: 81% of calories from fat. Air-fried: 14%.

Egg rolls are traditionally deep-fried until crisp and hot. And they usually contain lots of shrimp, which is high in sodium. Let's omit the shrimp and use healthy vegetables in this easy lunch recipe.

1 In a medium bowl, mix the yellow squash, carrot, red bell pepper, scallions, and soy sauce.

2 Place the egg roll wrappers on a work surface. Top each with about 3 tablespoons of the vegetable mixture.

3 In a small bowl, thoroughly mix the cornstarch and egg. Brush some egg mixture on the edges of each wrapper. Roll up the wrappers, folding over the sides so the filling is contained. Brush the egg mixture on the outside of each egg roll.

4 Air-fry for 7 to 10 minutes, or until brown and crunchy. Serve immediately.

INGREDIENT TIP Watch out for the sodium in egg roll wrappers. Some brands are loaded with salt, while others have no salt added at all. Wing's Egg Roll Wraps were used in the nutrition calculations for this recipe. Always read labels on any packaged or processed foods.

PER SERVING (1 egg roll) Calories: 130; Fat: 2g (14% of calories from fat); Saturated Fat: 0g; Protein: 6g; Carbohydrates: 23g; Sodium: 126mg; Fiber: 3g; Sugar: 4g; 56% DV vitamin A; 65% DV vitamin C

Grilled Cheese and Greens Sandwiches

PREP 15 minutes / **COOK** 6 to 8 minutes / **SERVES** 4

400°F

Vegetarian

1½ cups chopped mixed greens (kale, chard, collards; see Tip)

2 garlic cloves, thinly sliced

2 teaspoons olive oil

2 slices low-sodium low-fat Swiss cheese

4 slices low-sodium whole-wheat bread

Olive oil spray, for coating the sandwiches

A gooey grilled cheese sandwich is a quick and favorite lunch—but full of fat, calories, and sodium. This tasty take on a lunch standard cuts down on the cheese and adds quickly sautéed greens and veggies to boost the nutritional content.

1 In a 6-by-2-inch pan, mix the greens, garlic, and olive oil. Cook in the air fryer for 4 to 5 minutes, stirring once, until the vegetables are tender. Drain, if necessary.

2 Make 2 sandwiches, dividing half of the greens and 1 slice of Swiss cheese between 2 slices of bread. Lightly spray the outsides of the sandwiches with olive oil spray.

3 Grill the sandwiches in the air fryer for 6 to 8 minutes, turning with tongs halfway through, until the bread is toasted and the cheese melts.

4 Cut each sandwich in half to serve.

PREPARATION TIP To wash the greens, place the leaves in a sink filled with cold water and swish them around. Greens can be sandy, and this method lets the sand drop to the bottom of the sink.

PER SERVING (½ sandwich) Calories: 176; Fat: 6g (35% of calories from fat); Saturated Fat: 4g; Protein: 10g; Carbohydrates: 24g; Sodium: 139mg; Fiber: 5g; Sugar: 4g; 14% DV vitamin A; 9% DV vitamin C

Veggie Tuna Melts

PREP 15 minutes / **COOK** 7 to 11 minutes / **SERVES** 4

340°F

Family Favorite

2 low-sodium whole-wheat English muffins, split

1 (6-ounce) can chunk light low-sodium tuna, drained

1 cup shredded carrot

⅓ cup chopped mushrooms

2 scallions, white and green parts, sliced

⅓ cup nonfat Greek yogurt

2 tablespoons low-sodium stone-ground mustard

2 slices low-sodium low-fat Swiss cheese, halved

Open-faced sandwiches, like this veggie tuna combination and California Melts (page 42), are low in sodium and carbohydrates and focus your attention on the melty good fillings. Using whole-wheat English muffins here adds flavor and texture to this sandwich.

1 Place the English muffin halves in the air fryer basket. Grill for 3 to 4 minutes, or until crisp. Remove from the basket and set aside.

2 In a medium bowl, thoroughly mix the tuna, carrot, mushrooms, scallions, yogurt, and mustard. Top each half of the muffins with one-fourth of the tuna mixture and a half slice of Swiss cheese.

3 Grill in the air fryer for 4 to 7 minutes, or until the tuna mixture is hot and the cheese melts and starts to brown. Serve immediately.

SUBSTITUTION TIP You can use just about any vegetable you like on this delicious sandwich. Try chopped zucchini or yellow summer squash, or use bell peppers.

PER SERVING Calories: 191; Fat: 4g (19% of calories from fat); Saturated Fat: 2g; Protein: 23g; Carbohydrates: 16g; Sodium: 99mg; Fiber: 3g; Sugar: 5g; 130% DV vitamin A; 10% DV vitamin C

California Melts

PREP 10 minutes / **COOK** 3 to 4 minutes / **SERVES** 4

390°F

Fast, Vegetarian

2 low-sodium whole-wheat English muffins, split

2 tablespoons nonfat Greek yogurt

8 fresh baby spinach leaves

1 ripe tomato, cut into 4 slices

½ ripe avocado, peeled, pitted, and sliced lengthwise (see Tip)

8 fresh basil leaves

4 tablespoons crumbled fat-free low-sodium feta cheese, divided

Melt sandwiches are open-faced and topped with meats, vegetables, and cheeses. This recipe version uses foods that California is famous for—tomatoes and avocados. This is a super-quick recipe that makes lunch seem like a sunny, nutritious California dream.

1 Put the English muffin halves into the air fryer. Toast for 2 minutes, or until light golden brown. Transfer to a work surface.

2 Spread each muffin half with 1½ teaspoons of yogurt.

3 Top each muffin half with 2 spinach leaves, 1 tomato slice, one-fourth of the avocado, and 2 basil leaves. Sprinkle each with 1 tablespoon of feta cheese.

4 Toast the sandwiches in the air fryer for 3 to 4 minutes, or until the cheese softens and the sandwich is hot. Serve immediately.

INGREDIENT TIP Ripe avocados can be hard to find in the grocery store, so it helps to plan ahead for this recipe. Hass avocados, with the dark pebbly skin, have the best texture. Let the avocados ripen at room temperature for 2 or 3 days, or until they give slightly when pressed with your fingers.

PER SERVING Calories: 110; Fat: 3g (24% of calories from fat); Saturated Fat: 1g; Protein: 8g; Carbohydrates: 13g; Sodium: 98mg; Fiber: 3g; Sugar: 3g; 46% DV vitamin A; 21% DV vitamin C

Vegetable Pita Sandwiches

PREP 15 minutes / **COOK** 9 to 12 minutes / **SERVES** 4

390°F

Vegetarian, Very Low Sodium

1 baby eggplant, peeled and chopped (see Tip)

1 red bell pepper, sliced

½ cup diced red onion

½ cup shredded carrot

1 teaspoon olive oil

⅓ cup low-fat Greek yogurt

½ teaspoon dried tarragon

2 low-sodium whole-wheat pita breads, halved crosswise

Roasted vegetables make a delicious filling for pita sandwiches. These sandwiches are heated in the air fryer to toast the bread. You can use leftover roasted vegetables in this sandwich. Feel free to substitute your favorites.

1 In a 6-by-2-inch pan, stir together the eggplant, red bell pepper, red onion, carrot, and olive oil. Put the vegetable mixture into the air fryer basket and roast for 7 to 9 minutes, stirring once, until the vegetables are tender. Drain if necessary.

2 In a small bowl, thoroughly mix the yogurt and tarragon until well combined.

3 Stir the yogurt mixture into the vegetables. Stuff one-fourth of this mixture into each pita pocket.

4 Place the sandwiches in the air fryer and cook for 2 to 3 minutes, or until the bread is toasted. Serve immediately.

INGREDIENT TIP Baby eggplant is relatively new to the market; it is tender and sweet. If you can't find one, use 1 cup regular peeled, chopped eggplant.

PER SERVING Calories: 176; Fat: 4g (20% of calories from fat); Saturated Fat: 0g; Protein: 7g; Carbohydrates: 27g; Sodium: 22mg; Fiber: 3g; Sugar: 5g; 23% DV vitamin A; 30% DV vitamin C

Falafel

PREP 10 minutes / **COOK** 11 to 13 minutes / **MAKES** 12 falafel balls

380°F

Vegan, Very Low Sodium

1 (16-ounce) can no-salt-added chickpeas, rinsed and drained

⅓ cup whole-wheat pastry flour

⅓ cup minced red onion

2 garlic cloves, minced

2 tablespoons minced fresh cilantro

1 tablespoon olive oil

½ teaspoon ground cumin

¼ teaspoon cayenne pepper

AREN'T YOU GLAD YOU DIDN'T DEEP-FRY
You're consuming 12.5 fewer grams of fat. Congratulations.

Falafel is a deep-fried Middle Eastern mixture of chickpeas and seasonings. It is a typical street food stuffed in pita bread with vegetables. These falafel balls are easily made in the air fryer and are healthy and delicious when cooked this way.

1 In a medium bowl, mash the chickpeas with a potato masher until mostly smooth.

2 Stir in the pastry flour, red onion, garlic, cilantro, olive oil, cumin, and cayenne until well mixed. Form the chickpea mixture into 12 balls.

3 Air-fry the falafel balls, in batches, for 11 to 13 minutes, or until the falafel are firm and light golden brown. Serve.

SERVING TIP Serve these on a bed of mixed lettuces drizzled with yogurt mixed with cayenne pepper. Or stuff them into pita pockets with lettuce, Greek yogurt, chopped tomatoes, bell peppers, and more red onion.

PER SERVING (3 falafel balls) Calories: 172; Fat: 5g (26% of calories from fat); Saturated Fat: 1g; Protein: 7g; Carbohydrates: 25g; Sodium: 6mg; Fiber: 5g; Sugar: 2g; 2% DV vitamin A; 9% DV vitamin C

Stuffed Portobello Mushrooms

PREP 15 minutes / **COOK** 9 to 12 minutes / **SERVES** 4

390°F

Vegetarian

4 portobello mushrooms, wiped clean with a damp cloth, stemmed, and gills removed (see Tip)

1 teaspoon olive oil

2 cups chopped fresh baby spinach

1 red bell pepper, chopped

⅓ cup chopped red onion

⅓ cup nonfat Greek yogurt

2 tablespoons nonfat cream cheese, at room temperature

2 tablespoons grated Parmesan cheese

Portobello mushrooms are large, meaty fungi that are easy to stuff with just about anything—usually sausage, bacon, and cheese. This version is stuffed with lots of vegetables to make a savory and delicious light lunch.

1 Rub the mushrooms with the olive oil. Place them in the air fryer basket, hollow-side up, and air-fry for 3 minutes.

2 Carefully remove the mushroom caps because they will contain liquid. Drain the liquid out of the caps.

3 In a medium bowl, thoroughly mix the spinach, red bell pepper, red onion, yogurt, cream cheese, and Parmesan cheese. Stuff one-fourth of this mixture into each drained mushroom cap. Return the caps to the air fryer basket.

4 Air-fry for 6 to 9 minutes, or until the filling is hot and the mushroom caps are tender. Serve.

SUBSTITUTION TIP Portobello mushrooms are usually 3 to 4 inches in diameter. If you can't find them, use 4 large button mushrooms.

PER SERVING Calories: 100; Fat: 3g (27% of calories from fat); Saturated Fat: 1g; Protein: 9g; Carbohydrates: 13g; Sodium: 133mg; Fiber 2g; Sugar: 7g; 53% DV vitamin A; 132% DV vitamin C

Stuffed Tomatoes

PREP 10 minutes / **COOK** 16 to 20 minutes / **SERVES** 4

350°F

Gluten-Free, Vegetarian

4 medium beefsteak
tomatoes, rinsed and
patted dry

1 medium onion, chopped

½ cup grated carrot

1 garlic clove, minced

2 teaspoons olive oil

2 cups fresh baby spinach

¼ cup crumbled low-sodium
feta cheese

½ teaspoon dried basil

A classic! Firm beefsteak tomatoes hold their shape
when baked and are delicious stuffed with a cheesy
vegetable mixture. Make sure the tomatoes you buy
fit into the air fryer so you can cook all four at once.
This makes a tasty lunch or side dish.

1 Cut about ½ inch off the top of each tomato. Gently hollow
them out (see Tip), leaving a wall about ½ inch thick. Drain
the tomatoes, upside down, on paper towels while you prepare the filling.

2 In a 6-by-2-inch pan, mix the onion, carrot, garlic, and
olive oil. Bake for 4 to 6 minutes, or until the vegetables are
crisp-tender.

3 Stir in the spinach, feta cheese, and basil.

4 Fill each tomato with one-fourth of the vegetable mixture. Bake the tomatoes in the air fryer basket for 12 to
14 minutes, or until hot and tender. Serve immediately.

PREPARATION TIP To remove the center from each tomato,
a melon baller may help. Work carefully so you don't pierce the
tomato shell.

PER SERVING Calories: 79; Fat: 3g (34% of calories from fat); Saturated
Fat: 1g; Protein: 3g; Carbohydrates: 9g; Sodium: 136mg; Fiber: 1g; Sugar: 4g;
50% DV vitamin A; 53% DV vitamin C

Loaded Mini Potatoes

PREP 5 minutes / **COOK** 20 to 25 minutes / **SERVES** 4

360°F

Family Favorite, Vegetarian, Very Low Sodium

24 small new potatoes, or creamer potatoes, rinsed, scrubbed, and patted dry

1 teaspoon olive oil

½ cup low-fat Greek yogurt

1 tablespoon low-sodium stone-ground mustard (see Tip)

½ teaspoon dried basil

3 Roma tomatoes, seeded and chopped

2 scallions, white and green parts, chopped

2 tablespoons chopped fresh chives

AREN'T YOU GLAD YOU DIDN'T DEEP-FRY

A triple winner: calories dropped by 696, fat by 30 grams, and sodium by 767 milligrams!

Potato skins take a long time to cook, even in the air fryer. You must first roast the potatoes, then cool them, cut them into pieces, scoop out the flesh, add the toppings, and roast the potatoes again. This recipe simplifies things by roasting new potatoes, smashing them, and adding the toppings. It's a delicious lunch that's ready in 30 minutes.

1 In a large bowl, toss the potatoes with the olive oil. Transfer to the air fryer basket. Roast for 20 to 25 minutes, shaking the basket once, until the potatoes are crisp on the outside and tender within.

2 Meanwhile, in a small bowl, stir together the yogurt, mustard, and basil.

3 Place the potatoes on a serving platter and carefully smash each one slightly with the bottom of a drinking glass.

4 Top the potatoes with the yogurt mixture. Sprinkle with the tomatoes, scallions, and chives. Serve immediately.

INGREDIENT TIP Stone-ground mustard has some visible mustard seeds. They add interest and texture to this dish, but use any mustard you like.

PER SERVING Calories: 100; Fat: 2g (18% of calories from fat); Saturated Fat: 0g; Protein: 5g; Carbohydrates: 19g; Sodium: 33mg; Fiber: 2g; Sugar: 4g; 21% DV vitamin A; 59% DV vitamin C

Crustless Veggie Quiche

PREP 8 minutes / **COOK** 18 to 22 minutes / **SERVES** 3

320°F

Gluten-Free, Vegetarian

4 egg whites

1 egg

1 cup frozen chopped spinach, thawed and drained

1 red bell pepper, chopped

½ cup chopped mushrooms

⅓ cup minced red onion

1 tablespoon low-sodium mustard

1 slice low-sodium low-fat Swiss cheese, torn into small pieces

Nonstick cooking spray with flour, for greasing the pan

A crustless quiche is simple to make because you don't have to make pastry. This healthy and very-low-calorie quiche is packed full of nutritious vegetables, and it's so delicious. Enjoy it for breakfast or a light lunch.

1 In a medium bowl, beat the egg whites and egg until blended.

2 Stir in the spinach, red bell pepper, mushrooms, onion, and mustard.

3 Mix in the Swiss cheese.

4 Spray a 6-by-2-inch pan with nonstick cooking spray.

5 Pour the egg mixture into the prepared pan.

6 Bake for 18 to 22 minutes, or until the egg mixture is puffed, light golden brown, and set. Cool for 5 minutes before serving.

VARIATION If you want a crust, line the pan with piecrust dough. Prick the dough with a fork and bake for 4 to 6 minutes until firm. Continue with the recipe as directed.

PER SERVING Calories: 76; Fat: 3g (35% of calories from fat); Saturated Fat: 1g; Protein: 8g; Carbohydrates: 4g; Sodium: 102mg; Fiber: 1g; Sugar: 2g; 59% DV vitamin A; 28% DV vitamin C

Scrambled Eggs with Broccoli and Spinach

PREP 12 minutes / **COOK** 12 to 18 minutes / **SERVES** 4

350°F

Gluten-Free

2 teaspoons unsalted butter

1 medium onion, chopped

1 red bell pepper, chopped

1 cup small broccoli florets

½ teaspoon dried marjoram

6 egg whites

2 eggs

1 cup fresh baby spinach

Eggs aren't just for breakfast; they make a great lunch, too. Plentiful vegetables make this colorful recipe delicious and nutritious. To make the best scrambled eggs in the air fryer, they must be stirred three times while cooking.

1 In a 6-by-2-inch pan in the air fryer, heat the butter for 1 minute, or until it melts.

2 Add the onion, red bell pepper, broccoli, marjoram, and 1 tablespoon of water. Air-fry for 3 to 5 minutes, or until the vegetables are crisp-tender. Drain, if necessary.

3 Meanwhile, in a medium bowl, beat the egg whites and eggs until frothy.

4 Add the spinach and eggs to the vegetables in the pan. Air-fry for 8 to 12 minutes, stirring three times during cooking, until the eggs are set and fluffy and reach 160°F on a meat thermometer. Serve immediately.

SUBSTITUTION TIP Get creative with the vegetables in this recipe. Sliced or chopped mushrooms are good, as are cauliflower florets, zucchini, or yellow summer squash.

PER SERVING Calories: 86; Fat: 3g (32% of calories from fat); Saturated Fat: 1g; Protein: 8g; Carbohydrates: 5g; Sodium: 116mg; Fiber: 1g; Sugar: 3g; 25% DV vitamin A; 47% DV vitamin C

Beans and Greens Pizza

PREP 11 minutes / **COOK** 14 to 19 minutes / **SERVES** 4

350°F

Vegetarian

¾ cup whole-wheat pastry flour

½ teaspoon low-sodium baking powder

1 tablespoon olive oil, divided

1 cup chopped kale

2 cups chopped fresh baby spinach

1 cup canned no-salt-added cannellini beans, rinsed and drained

½ teaspoon dried thyme

1 piece low-sodium string cheese, torn into pieces

This easy pizza uses a simple and quick homemade crust made with baking powder so you don't have to wait for the yeast to rise. It's topped with sautéed greens and cannellini beans for an unusual pizza with lots of flavor.

1 In a small bowl, mix the pastry flour and baking powder until well combined.

2 Add ¼ cup of water and 2 teaspoons of olive oil. Mix until a dough forms.

3 On a floured surface, press or roll the dough into a 7-inch round. Set aside while you cook the greens.

4 In a 6-by-2-inch pan, mix the kale, spinach, and remaining teaspoon of the olive oil. Air-fry for 3 to 5 minutes, until the greens are wilted. Drain well.

5 Put the pizza dough into the air fryer basket. Top with the greens, cannellini beans, thyme, and string cheese. Air-fry for 11 to 14 minutes, or until the crust is golden brown and the cheese is melted. Cut into quarters to serve.

SUBSTITUTION TIP Use any type of greens and any type of canned bean in this easy recipe. Cook the greens before you top the pizza because they contain a lot of moisture that will make the crust soggy.

PER SERVING Calories: 175; Fat: 5g (25% of calories from fat); Saturated Fat: 1g; Protein: 9g; Carbohydrates: 24g; Sodium: 106mg; Fiber: 7g; Sugar: 0g; 62% DV vitamin A; 45% DV vitamin C

Grilled Chicken Mini Pizzas

PREP 15 minutes / **COOK** 3 to 6 minutes / **SERVES** 4

360°F

Family Favorite

2 low-sodium whole-wheat pita breads, split (see Tip)

½ cup no-salt-added tomato sauce

1 garlic clove, minced

½ teaspoon dried oregano

1 cooked shredded chicken breast

1 cup chopped button mushrooms

½ cup chopped red bell pepper

½ cup shredded part skim low-sodium mozzarella cheese

Craving pizza? You're in luck—mini pizzas cook so beautifully in the air fryer. The crust becomes very crisp, and the toppings melt to perfection. This healthy recipe uses whole-wheat pita bread for the crust, topped with veggies, cooked chicken, and a bit of cheese. Enjoy one with a green salad for a satisfying lunch.

1 Place the pita breads, insides up, on a work surface.

2 In a small bowl, stir together the tomato sauce, garlic, and oregano. Spread about 2 tablespoons of the sauce over each pita half.

3 Top each with ¼ cup of shredded chicken, ¼ cup of mushrooms, and 2 tablespoons of red bell pepper. Sprinkle with the mozzarella cheese.

4 Bake the pizzas for 3 to 6 minutes, or until the cheese melts and starts to brown and the pita bread is crisp. Serve immediately.

PREPARATION TIP To split pita breads, use kitchen scissors and make a cut along the edge. Carefully cut the two halves of the pita apart, following the natural seam.

PER SERVING Calories: 249; Fat: 7g (25% of calories from fat); Saturated Fat: 3g; Protein: 23g; Carbohydrates: 25g; Sodium: 128mg; Fiber: 3g; Sugar: 3g; 17% DV vitamin A; 64% DV vitamin C

Chicken Croquettes

PREP 15 minutes / **COOK** 7 to 10 minutes / **MAKES** 8 croquettes

370°F

2 (5-ounce) cooked chicken breasts, finely chopped (see Tip)

⅓ cup low-fat Greek yogurt

3 tablespoons minced red onion

2 celery stalks, minced

1 garlic clove, minced

½ teaspoon dried basil

2 egg whites, divided

2 slices low-sodium whole-wheat bread, crumbled

AREN'T YOU GLAD YOU DIDN'T DEEP-FRY
Your heart thanks you for eating 639 fewer milligrams of sodium.

This old-fashioned dish is a great way to use up left-over chicken. Chop the chicken very finely and mix it with vegetables and Greek yogurt to make little balls that become light and crisp when cooked in the air fryer. Serve these croquettes on a green salad for a simple yet tasty lunch.

1 In a medium bowl, thoroughly mix the chicken, yogurt, red onion, celery, garlic, basil, and 1 egg white. Form the mixture into 8 ovals and gently press into shape.

2 In a shallow bowl, beat the remaining egg white until foamy.

3 Put the bread crumbs on a plate.

4 Dip the chicken croquettes into the egg white and then into the bread crumbs to coat.

5 Air-fry the croquettes, in batches, for 7 to 10 minutes, or until the croquettes reach an internal temperature of 160°F on a meat thermometer and their color is golden brown. Serve immediately.

SUBSTITUTION TIP You could make these croquettes with 2 cups finely chopped shrimp or cooked crabmeat instead of chicken. Be aware, though, that the sodium content will increase.

PER SERVING (2 croquettes) Calories: 207, Fat: 4g (17% of calories from fat); Saturated Fat: 2g; Protein: 32g; Carbohydrates: 8g, Sodium: 126mg; Fiber: 1g; Sugar: 2g; 5% DV vitamin A; 2% DV vitamin C

Chicken and Fruit Bruschetta

PREP 15 minutes / **COOK** 5 to 10 minutes / **SERVES** 4

350°F

1 tablespoon unsalted butter, at room temperature

3 slices low-sodium whole-wheat bread

½ cup chopped peeled peaches

½ cup chopped fresh strawberries

½ cup fresh blueberries

¼ cup canned low-sodium chicken breast, drained

1 tablespoon freshly squeezed lemon juice

1 tablespoon honey

Bruschetta is an Italian term that means "to roast over coals." This recipe is made from toasted bread topped with any number of ingredients—here, chicken and fresh fruit—and is baked or broiled. This makes a delightful summer lunch on the patio.

1 Spread the butter on the bread and place it in the air fryer basket. Bake for 3 to 5 minutes, or until light golden brown.

2 Meanwhile, in a small bowl, gently mix the peaches, strawberries, blueberries, chicken, and lemon juice.

3 Remove the bread from the basket. Top each slice with one-third of the chicken mixture. Drizzle with the honey. Return to the basket, in batches, and bake for 2 to 5 minutes, until the fruit starts to caramelize.

4 Cut each slice into quarters and serve immediately.

SUBSTITUTION TIP You can use other fruits in this recipe, but they may need to be cooked first. Sauté some apples or pears in the air fryer before you use them, or try chopped nectarines or plums.

PER SERVING (3 bruschetta) Calories: 175; Fat: 4g (21% of calories from fat); Saturated Fat: 3g; Protein: 9g; Carbohydrates: 30g; Sodium: 121mg; Fiber: 4g; Sugar: 15g; DV vitamin A; 47% DV vitamin C

Kale Chips with Tex-Mex Dip, p. 56

Four

APPETIZERS

Kale Chips with Tex-Mex Dip

PREP 10 minutes / **COOK** 5 to 6 minutes / **SERVES** 8

390°F

Gluten-Free, Vegetarian, Fast

1 cup Greek yogurt

1 tablespoon chili powder

⅓ cup low-sodium salsa, well drained

1 bunch curly kale

1 teaspoon olive oil

¼ teaspoon coarse sea salt

AREN'T YOU GLAD YOU DIDN'T DEEP-FRY

Deep-fried kale chips contain a whopping 40% calories from fat.

Kale chips are nothing new, of course. But making them in the air fryer is! As good as kale is for you, deep-frying it just adds lots of fat and calories. The crisp and airy chips are served with a delicious dip flavored with Tex-Mex ingredients.

1 In a small bowl, combine the yogurt, chili powder, and drained salsa; refrigerate.

2 Rinse the kale thoroughly, and pat dry. Remove the stems and ribs from the kale, using a sharp knife. Cut or tear the leaves into 3-inch pieces.

3 Toss the kale with the olive oil in a large bowl.

4 Air-fry the kale in small batches until the leaves are crisp. This should take 5 to 6 minutes. Shake the basket once during cooking time.

5 As you remove the kale chips, sprinkle them with a bit of the sea salt.

6 When all of the kale chips are done, serve with the dip.

SUBSTITUTION TIP Any dip made with Greek yogurt would be delicious with the kale chips. You could add lots of fresh herbs such as dill or thyme, or add some pesto.

PER SERVING Calories: 35; Fat: 1g (26% calories from fat); Saturated Fat: 0g; Protein: 4g; Carbohydrates: 2g; Sodium: 105mg; Fiber: 1g; Sugar: 2g; 125% DV vitamin A; 13% DV vitamin C

Spicy Sweet Potato Fries

PREP 15 minutes / **COOK** 8 to 12 minutes / **SERVES** 4

390°F

Family Favorite, Gluten-Free, Vegetarian

2 large sweet potatoes, peeled and cut into ⅓-by-⅓-inch sticks

1 teaspoon ground cumin

1 teaspoon ground paprika

½ teaspoon garlic powder

½ teaspoon cayenne pepper

⅛ teaspoon freshly ground black pepper

1 cup low-fat Greek yogurt

2 teaspoons olive oil

AREN'T YOU GLAD YOU DIDN'T DEEP-FRY

You saved 13 grams of fat.

Sweet potato fries might be a new—and oh so tasty—experience for those who have eaten fries made only with russet potatoes. They are crisp and tender and have a pleasingly sweet flavor—and they are packed with vitamin A! Serve with a creamy dip made from Greek yogurt and loads of spices.

1 In a medium bowl of cold water, soak the sweet potato sticks and set them aside while you make the dip.

2 In a small bowl, mix the cumin, paprika, garlic powder, cayenne, and black pepper.

3 In another small bowl, whisk half the spice mixture with the yogurt. Refrigerate.

4 Drain the sweet potatoes, pat them dry, and place them in a large bowl. Sprinkle them with the olive oil. Toss for 1 minute to coat thoroughly.

5 Sprinkle the fries with the remaining spice mixture and toss again to coat. Transfer the potatoes to the air fryer basket. Air-fry for 8 to 12 minutes, or until crisp, hot, and golden brown, shaking the basket once during cooking.

6 Transfer to a serving dish. Serve with the dip.

SUBSTITUTION TIP Use other seasonings as you like, such as curry powder for a change of pace or a combination of dried herbs.

PER SERVING Calories: 125; Fat: 4g (29% of calories from fat); Saturated Fat: 1g; Protein: 7g; Carbohydrates: 17g; Sodium: 73mg; Fiber: 2g; Sugar: 5g; 198% DV vitamin A; 9% DV vitamin C

Purple Potato Chips with Chipotle Sauce and Rosemary

PREP 20 minutes / COOK 9 to 14 minutes / SERVES 6

400°F

Gluten Free, Vegetarian

1 cup Greek yogurt

2 chipotle chiles, minced

2 tablespoons adobo sauce

1 teaspoon paprika

1 tablespoon lemon juice

10 purple fingerling potatoes

1 teaspoon olive oil

2 teaspoons minced fresh rosemary leaves

⅛ teaspoon cayenne pepper

¼ teaspoon coarse sea salt

AREN'T YOU GLAD YOU DIDN'T DEEP-FRY
Deep-fried potato chips contain at least 40% calories from fat.

Have you tried the purple potatoes that are now in most grocery stores? They are really purple inside, so they are a fun food to serve at parties. This recipe is made with fingerling potatoes, which are shaped like, well, fingers! These chips are served with a delicious and spicy sauce made with chipotle chiles, which are smoked jalapeños packed in a spicy red sauce.

1 In a medium bowl, combine the yogurt, minced chiles, adobo sauce, paprika, and lemon juice. Mix well and refrigerate.

2 Wash the potatoes and dry them with paper towels. Slice the potatoes lengthwise, as thinly as possible. You can use a mandoline, a vegetable peeler, or a very sharp knife.

3 Combine the potato slices in a medium bowl and drizzle with the olive oil; toss to coat.

4 Cook the chips, in batches, in the air fryer basket, for 9 to 14 minutes. Use tongs to gently rearrange the chips halfway during cooking time.

5 Sprinkle the chips with the rosemary, cayenne pepper, and sea salt. Serve with the chipotle sauce for dipping.

INGREDIENT TIP Purple potatoes are high in antioxidants, compounds that help prevent inflammation and may help protect you against disease. In particular, they contain chlorogenic acid, which may help reduce blood pressure.

PER SERVING Calories: 68; Fat: 1g (13% calories from fat); Saturated Fat: 0g; Protein 4g; Carbohydrates 11g; Sodium 112mg; Fiber 1g; Sugar 2g; 0% DV vitamin A; 17% DV vitamin C

Cinnamon-Pear Chips

PREP 15 minutes / **COOK** 9 to 13 minutes / **SERVES** 4

380°F

Gluten-Free,
No Sodium, Vegan

2 firm Bosc pears,
cut crosswise into
⅛-inch-thick slices
(see Tip)

1 tablespoon freshly
squeezed lemon juice

½ teaspoon ground
cinnamon

⅛ teaspoon ground
cardamom or ground nutmeg

Chips made from thinly sliced pears make a slightly sweet, healthy snack. Best news? These chips have no fat and no sodium. Serve them alone or with a dip made from Greek yogurt, pear jam, and applesauce.

1 Separate the smaller stem-end pear rounds from the larger rounds with seeds. Remove the core and seeds from the larger slices. Sprinkle all slices with lemon juice, cinnamon, and cardamom.

2 Put the smaller chips into the air fryer basket. Air-fry for 3 to 5 minutes, until light golden brown, shaking the basket once during cooking. Remove from the air fryer.

3 Repeat with the larger slices, air-frying for 6 to 8 minutes, until light golden brown, shaking the basket once during cooking.

4 Remove the chips from the air fryer. Cool and serve or store in an airtight container at room temperature up for to 2 days.

SUBSTITUTION TIP Make this recipe with apples. Peel the apples, remove the core, and cut into thin slices. Air-fry for 7 to 9 minutes.

PER SERVING Calories: 30; Fat: 0g (0% calories from fat); Saturated Fat: 0g; Protein: 7g; Carbohydrates: 8g; Sodium: 0mg; Fiber: 2g; Sugar: 5g; 5% DV vitamin C

Hearty Greens Chips
with Curried Yogurt Sauce

PREP 10 minutes / **COOK** 5 to 6 minutes / **SERVES** 4

390°F

Gluten-Free, Vegetarian

1 cup low-fat Greek yogurt

1 tablespoon freshly squeezed lemon juice

1 tablespoon curry powder

½ bunch curly kale, stemmed, ribs removed and discarded, leaves cut into 2- to 3-inch pieces

½ bunch chard, stemmed, ribs removed and discarded, leaves cut into 2- to 3-inch pieces

1½ teaspoons olive oil

AREN'T YOU GLAD YOU DIDN'T DEEP-FRY

When fried, 98% of the calories come from fat . . . seriously bad for you.

"Chips" made from sturdy leafy greens have become popular during the last few years. You can make these satisfying snacks from kale, mustard greens, chard, or even beet greens. The greens are loaded with nutrients, including vitamins C, K, and A, and lots of fiber that can help protect your heart and prevent colon cancer. These are delicious served with this curried dip.

1 In a small bowl, stir together the yogurt, lemon juice, and curry powder. Set aside.

2 In a large bowl, toss the kale and chard with the olive oil, working the oil into the leaves with your hands. This helps break up the fibers in the leaves so the chips are tender.

3 Air-fry the greens in batches for 5 to 6 minutes, until crisp, shaking the basket once during cooking. Serve with the yogurt sauce.

COOKING TIP Don't overcrowd the air fryer basket. The greens do contain a lot of water and need space for the liquid to evaporate.

PER SERVING Calories: 76; Fat: 2g (24% of calories from fat); Saturated Fat: 0g; Protein: 7g; Carbohydrates: 10g; Sodium: 91mg; Fiber: 1g; Sugar: 3g; 107% DV vitamin A; 64% DV vitamin C

Broccoli-Spinach Dip

PREP 10 minutes / **COOK** 9 to 14 minutes / **SERVES** 4

340°F

Gluten-Free, Vegetarian

½ cup low-fat Greek yogurt

¼ cup nonfat cream cheese

½ cup frozen chopped broccoli, thawed and drained

½ cup frozen chopped spinach, thawed and drained

⅓ cup chopped red bell pepper

1 garlic clove, minced

½ teaspoon dried oregano

2 tablespoons grated low-sodium Parmesan cheese

A hot dip is a great addition to any appetizer buffet or party menu. To keep the dip warm, transfer it to a small slow cooker or put it in a chafing dish. Serve this hearty dip with breadsticks (low-sodium please!), carrot sticks, and bell pepper strips.

1 In a medium bowl, blend the yogurt and cream cheese until well combined.

2 Stir in the broccoli, spinach, red bell pepper, garlic, and oregano. Transfer to a 6-by-2-inch pan.

3 Sprinkle with the Parmesan cheese.

4 Place the pan in the air fryer basket. Bake for 9 to 14 minutes, until the dip is bubbly and the top starts to brown. Serve immediately.

INGREDIENT TIP There are several kinds of frozen spinach on the market. You want chopped spinach for this dip because it blends better with the other ingredients.

PER SERVING Calories: 59; Fat: 1g (15% of calories from fat); Saturated Fat: 0g; Protein: 7g; Carbohydrates: 7g; Sodium: 130mg; Fiber: 1g; Sugar: 3g; 40% DV vitamin A; 59% DV vitamin C

Roasted Grape Dip

PREP 10 minutes / **COOK** 8 to 12 minutes / **SERVES** 6

380°F

Gluten-Free, Vegetarian, Very Low Sodium

2 cups seedless red grapes, rinsed and patted dry (see Tip)

1 tablespoon apple cider vinegar

1 tablespoon honey

1 cup low-fat Greek yogurt

2 tablespoons 2 percent milk

2 tablespoons minced fresh basil

Have you ever tried roasted grapes? Not only do they make a fabulous side dish to serve with chicken or pork, but when mixed with yogurt and basil, they also make a delectable dip to serve with crackers, apple slices, and pear slices.

1 In the air fryer basket, sprinkle the grapes with the cider vinegar and drizzle with the honey. Toss to coat. Roast the grapes for 8 to 12 minutes, or until shriveled but still soft. Remove from the air fryer.

2 In a medium bowl, stir together the yogurt and milk.

3 Gently blend in the grapes and basil. Serve immediately, or cover and chill for 1 to 2 hours.

INGREDIENT TIP Both red grapes and green grapes work well in this recipe—but remember that red grapes are better for you. They contain an antioxidant called quercetin that has anti-inflammatory properties.

PER SERVING Calories: 71; Fat: 0g; Saturated Fat: 0g; Protein: 4g; Carbohydrates: 15g; Sodium: 22mg; Fiber: 0g; Sugar: 13g; 2% DV vitamin A; 3% DV vitamin C

Phyllo Vegetable Triangles

PREP 15 minutes / **COOK** 6 to 11 minutes / **SERVES** 6

390°F

Family Favorite, Vegetarian

3 tablespoons minced onion

2 garlic cloves, minced

2 tablespoons grated carrot

1 teaspoon olive oil

3 tablespoons frozen baby peas, thawed

2 tablespoons nonfat cream cheese, at room temperature

6 sheets frozen phyllo dough, thawed (see Tip)

Olive oil spray, for coating the dough

AREN'T YOU GLAD YOU DIDN'T DEEP-FRY

You reduced your percentage of calories from fat by half—with no reduction in fun.

Phyllo, or filo, dough is a layered dough with lots of butter between layers that helps create a flaky texture. But you don't have to use butter—use olive oil spray! This crunchy little appetizer is fun to make and to serve.

1 In a 6-by-2-inch pan, combine the onion, garlic, carrot, and olive oil. Air-fry for 2 to 4 minutes, or until the vegetables are crisp-tender. Transfer to a bowl.

2 Stir in the peas and cream cheese to the vegetable mixture. Let cool while you prepare the dough.

3 Lay one sheet of phyllo on a work surface and lightly spray with olive oil spray. Top with another sheet of phyllo. Repeat with the remaining 4 phyllo sheets; you'll have 3 stacks with 2 layers each. Cut each stack lengthwise into 4 strips (12 strips total).

4 Place a scant 2 teaspoons of the filling near the bottom of each strip. Bring one corner up over the filling to make a triangle; continue folding the triangles over, as you would fold a flag. Seal the edge with a bit of water. Repeat with the remaining strips and filling.

5 Air-fry the triangles, in 2 batches, for 4 to 7 minutes, or until golden brown. Serve.

INGREDIENT TIP Some brands of phyllo will thaw at room temperature in a few minutes; others need to be thawed overnight in the refrigerator. Read package directions carefully.

PER SERVING Calories: 66; Fat: 2g (27% of calories from fat); Saturated Fat: 0g; Protein: 2g; Carbohydrates: 11g; Sodium: 121mg; Fiber: 1g; Sugar: 1g; 1% DV vitamin A; 2% DV vitamin C

Vegetable Pot Stickers

PREP 12 minutes / **COOK** 11 to 18 minutes / **MAKES** 12 pot stickers

370°F

Vegan

1 cup shredded red cabbage

¼ cup chopped button mushrooms

¼ cup grated carrot

2 tablespoons minced onion

2 garlic cloves, minced

2 teaspoons grated fresh ginger

12 gyoza/pot sticker wrappers (see Tip)

2½ teaspoons olive oil, divided

Pot stickers are little dumplings cooked until golden brown on the bottom. Water is added to the pan, and they are steamed until done. These tasty little bites are filled with sautéed vegetables and are easy to make in the air fryer.

1 In a 6-by-2-inch pan, combine the red cabbage, mushrooms, carrot, onion, garlic, and ginger. Add 1 tablespoon of water. Place in the air fryer and cook for 3 to 6 minutes, until the vegetables are crisp-tender. Drain and set aside.

2 Working one at a time, place the pot sticker wrappers on a work surface. Top each wrapper with a scant 1 tablespoon of the filling. Fold half of the wrapper over the other half to form a half circle. Dab one edge with water and press both edges together.

3 To another 6-by-2-inch pan, add 1¼ teaspoons of olive oil. Put half of the pot stickers, seam-side up, in the pan. Air-fry for 5 minutes, or until the bottoms are light golden brown. Add 1 tablespoon of water and return the pan to the air fryer.

4 Air-fry for 4 to 6 minutes more, or until hot. Repeat with the remaining pot stickers, remaining 1¼ teaspoons of oil, and another tablespoon of water. Serve immediately.

INGREDIENT TIP Substitute wonton wrappers for the gyoza/pot sticker wrappers if you can't find them, but watch out for the sodium content—read the labels to make sure there isn't too much.

PER SERVING (3 pot stickers) Calories: 87; Fat: 3g (31% of calories from fat); Saturated Fat: 0g; Protein: 2g; Carbohydrates: 14g; Sodium: 58mg; Fiber: 1g; Sugar: 1g; 5% DV vitamin A; 22% DV vitamin C

Roasted Mushrooms with Garlic

PREP 3 minutes / **COOK** 22 to 27 minutes / **SERVES** 4

350°F

Gluten-Free, Vegan,
Very Low Sodium

16 garlic cloves, peeled
(see Tip)

2 teaspoons olive oil, divided

16 button mushrooms

½ teaspoon dried marjoram

⅛ teaspoon freshly ground
black pepper

1 tablespoon white wine or
low-sodium vegetable broth

Roasted mushrooms are tender and meaty tasting. When cooked with whole garlic cloves, the flavor is incredibly fragrant. Serve this appetizer on toast points or in a dish with cocktail picks so your guests can easily spear the mushrooms and garlic cloves.

1 In a 6-by-2-inch pan, mix the garlic with 1 teaspoon of olive oil. Roast in the air fryer for 12 minutes.

2 Add the mushrooms, marjoram, and pepper. Stir to coat. Drizzle with the remaining 1 teaspoon of olive oil and the white wine.

3 Return to the air fryer and roast for 10 to 15 minutes more, or until the mushrooms and garlic cloves are tender. Serve.

INGREDIENT TIP Look for peeled, whole garlic cloves in the supermarket to save prep time. If you don't find them, to peel the cloves, press them with the side of a chef's knife to loosen the peel so it is easily removed.

PER SERVING Calories: 127; Fat: 4g (28% of calories from fat); Saturated Fat: 0g; Protein: 13g; Carbohydrates: 17g; Sodium: 20mg; Fiber: 4g; Sugar: 8g; 14% DV vitamin C

Southwest Stuffed Mushrooms

PREP 15 minutes / **COOK** 8 to 12 minutes / **SERVES** 4

350°F

Vegetarian, Very Low Sodium

16 medium button mushrooms, rinsed and patted dry

⅓ cup low-sodium salsa

3 garlic cloves, minced

1 medium onion, finely chopped

1 jalapeño pepper, minced (see Tip)

⅛ teaspoon cayenne pepper

3 tablespoons shredded pepper Jack cheese

2 teaspoons olive oil

AREN'T YOU GLAD YOU DIDN'T DEEP-FRY

Calories per serving are reduced by almost half!

Stuffed mushrooms are usually baked in the oven, but also sometimes deep-fried. Mushrooms are so mild and tender and can be stuffed with just about anything. The spicy ingredients in this dish will spice up your party.

1 Remove the stems from the mushrooms and finely chop them, reserving the whole caps.

2 In a medium bowl, mix the salsa, garlic, onion, jalapeño, cayenne, and pepper Jack cheese. Stir in the chopped mushroom stems.

3 Stuff this mixture into the mushroom caps, mounding the filling. Drizzle the olive oil on the mushrooms. Air-fry the mushrooms in the air fryer basket for 8 to 12 minutes, or until the filling is hot and the mushrooms are tender. Serve immediately.

INGREDIENT TIP   The seeds and membranes in a jalapeño are the spiciest part of this vegetable. Remove them for a milder dish, or leave them in for more heat.

PER SERVING Calories: 55; Fat: 2g (34% of calories from fat); Saturated Fat: 1g; Protein: 5g; Carbohydrates: 7g; Sodium: 8mg; Fiber: 1g; Sugar: 2g; 4% DV vitamin A; 10% DV vitamin C

Buffalo Cauliflower Snacks

PREP 15 minutes / **COOK** 5 minutes / **SERVES** 6

380°F

Family Favorite, Gluten-Free, Vegetarian

1 large head cauliflower, separated into small florets

1 tablespoon olive oil

½ teaspoon garlic powder

⅓ cup low-sodium hot wing sauce

⅔ cup nonfat Greek yogurt

½ teaspoons Tabasco sauce

1 celery stalk, chopped

1 tablespoon crumbled blue cheese

AREN'T YOU GLAD YOU DIDN'T DEEP-FRY

Your game plan to cut fat scored a 50% reduction.

Everyone knows Buffalo chicken wings—that deep-fried appetizer served with blue cheese sauce and loaded with fat and sodium. This version is made with cauliflower instead of chicken wings, and the dip is made with Greek yogurt, hot sauce, and just a bit of blue cheese. It's a winning recipe to serve while you're watching the game.

1 In a large bowl, toss the cauliflower florets with the olive oil. Sprinkle with the garlic powder and toss again to coat. Put half of the cauliflower in the air fryer basket. Air-fry for 5 to 7 minutes, until the cauliflower is browned, shaking the basket once during cooking.

2 Transfer to a serving bowl and toss with half of the wing sauce. Repeat with the remaining cauliflower and wing sauce.

3 In a small bowl, stir together the yogurt, Tabasco sauce, celery, and blue cheese. Serve with the cauliflower for dipping.

NUTRITION NOTE Cauliflower is one of the most nutritious vegetables. It is a member of the cruciferous family, which means it contains compounds that may help reduce your risk of developing cancer and other diseases.

PER SERVING Calories: 86; Fat: 3g (31% of calories from fat); Saturated Fat: 1g; Protein: 5g; Carbohydrates: 12g; Sodium: 79mg; Fiber: 4g; Sugar: 6g; 112% DV vitamin C

Glazed Chicken Wings

PREP 5 minutes / **COOK** 25 minutes / **SERVES** 4

390°F

Family Favorite, Gluten Free

8 chicken wings

3 tablespoons honey

1 tablespoons lemon juice

1 tablespoon low-sodium chicken stock

2 cloves garlic, minced

¼ cup thinly sliced green onion

¾ cup low-sodium barbecue sauce

4 stalks celery, cut into pieces

AREN'T YOU GLAD YOU DIDN'T DEEP-FRY

Deep-fried chicken wings can contain more than 60% calories from fat.

Chicken wings make a great appetizer for serving during a big game, or an easy lunch or light dinner. They are tossed in a honey and lemon sauce to give them wonderful flavor and a light glaze. The wings are served with a low sodium barbecue sauce for even more flavor.

1 Pat the chicken wings dry. Cut off the small end piece and discard or freeze it to make chicken stock later.

2 Put the wings into the air fryer basket. Air fry for 20 minutes, shaking the basket twice while cooking.

3 Meanwhile, combine the honey, lemon juice, chicken stock, and garlic, and whisk until combined.

4 Remove the wings from the air fryer and put into a 6" x 2" pan. Pour the sauce over the wings and toss gently to coat.

5 Return the pan to the air fryer and air fry for another 4 to 5 minutes or until the wings are glazed and a food thermometer registers 165ºF. Sprinkle with the green onion and serve the wings with the barbecue sauce and celery.

INGREDIENT TIP You can sometimes buy "chicken drummettes" at the grocery store. They are made from the whole chicken wing and they do look like a little drumstick. Use about 12 in this recipe if you want to use that product.

PER SERVIING Calories: 287; Fat: 11g (35% of calories from fat); Saturated Fat: 3g; Protein: 16g; Carbohydrates: 30g; Sodium: 301mg; Fiber: 1g; Sugar: 23g; 18% DV vitamin A; 14% DV vitamin C

Mini Chicken Meatballs

PREP 10 minutes / **COOK** 13 to 20 minutes / **MAKES** 16 meatballs

370°F

Family Favorite

2 teaspoons olive oil

¼ cup minced onion

¼ cup minced red bell pepper

2 vanilla wafers, crushed

1 egg white

½ teaspoon dried thyme

½ pound ground chicken breast (see Tip)

AREN'T YOU GLAD YOU DIDN'T DEEP-FRY

These meatballs have 222 fewer calories and 22 percent fewer fat calories.

Meatballs make a great appetizer. These little bites are made from ground chicken, so they are automatically lower in fat than those made with ground beef. The vanilla wafers add a slightly floral note and are delicious. You could also add a sauce made from yogurt and spices or heat up marinara sauce for dipping.

1 In a 6-by-2-inch pan, mix the olive oil, onion, and red bell pepper. Put the pan in the air fryer. Cook for 3 to 5 minutes, or until the vegetables are tender.

2 In a medium bowl, mix the cooked vegetables, crushed wafers, egg white, and thyme until well combined.

3 Mix in the chicken, gently but thoroughly, until everything is combined.

4 Form the mixture into 16 meatballs and place them in the air fryer basket. Air-fry for 10 to 15 minutes, or until the meatballs reach an internal temperature of 165°F on a meat thermometer. Serve immediately.

INGREDIENT TIP Don't buy ground chicken thighs or a combination of chicken thighs and breast meat unless you want to eat a lot more fat. Chicken breasts alone are very low in fat.

PER SERVING (4 meatballs) Calories: 98; Fat: 3g (28% of calories from fat); Saturated Fat: 0g; Protein: 14g; Carbohydrates: 4g; Sodium: 40mg; Fiber: 1g; Sugar: 3g; 6% DV vitamin A; 33% DV vitamin C

Vegetable Shrimp Toast

PREP 15 minutes / **COOK** 3 to 6 minutes / **SERVES** 4

350°F

8 large raw shrimp, peeled and finely chopped (see Tip)

1 egg white

2 garlic cloves, minced

3 tablespoons minced red bell pepper

1 medium celery stalk, minced

2 tablespoons cornstarch

¼ teaspoon Chinese five-spice powder

3 slices firm thin-sliced no-sodium whole-wheat bread

AREN'T YOU GLAD YOU DIDN'T DEEP-FRY
You (and your waistline) have 207 fewer calories on your plate.

Shrimp toast is a popular appetizer in Chinese restaurants. The traditional recipe includes chopped shrimp mixed with egg whites and seasonings that is spread on toast and deep-fried until crisp. This recipe uses whole-wheat bread and reduces the amount of shrimp to decrease the sodium level. Minced vegetables add color, texture, and nutrients.

1 In a small bowl, stir together the shrimp, egg white, garlic, red bell pepper, celery, cornstarch, and five-spice powder. Top each slice of bread with one-third of the shrimp mixture, spreading it evenly to the edges. With a sharp knife, cut each slice of bread into 4 strips.

2 Place the shrimp toasts in the air fryer basket in a single layer. You may need to cook them in batches. Air-fry for 3 to 6 minutes, until crisp and golden brown. Serve.

SUBSTITUTION TIP Substitute finely minced cooked crabmeat for the shrimp, or use ground chicken or ground turkey instead. There will be more sodium in the recipe if you use crabmeat, but less if you use ground chicken or ground turkey.

PER SERVING (3 toasts) Calories: 110; Fat: 2g (16% of calories from fat); Saturated Fat: 0g; Protein: 9g; Carbohydrates: 15g; Sodium: 139mg; Fiber: 2g; Sugar: 1g; 6% DV vitamin A; 24% DV vitamin C

Salmon Nachos

PREP 10 minutes / COOK 9 to 12 minutes / SERVES 6

360°F

Gluten-Free

2 ounces (about 36) baked
no-salt corn tortilla chips
(see Tip)

1 (5-ounce) baked salmon
fillet, flaked

½ cup canned low-sodium
black beans, rinsed
and drained

1 red bell pepper, chopped

½ cup grated carrot

1 jalapeño pepper, minced

⅓ cup shredded low-sodium
low-fat Swiss cheese

1 tomato, chopped

Nachos are typically made with fried tortilla chips, topped with vegetables and lots of cheese, and baked until the chips are crisp and the cheese is melted. This appetizer (yes, delicious) has a lot of fat and not much nutritional value. For a healthier alternative, use baked tortilla chips, leftover cooked salmon, and plenty of vegetables to turn this snack into a guilt-free treat.

1 In a 6-by-2-inch pan, layer the tortilla chips. Top with the salmon, black beans, red bell pepper, carrot, jalapeño, and Swiss cheese.

2 Bake in the air fryer for 9 to 12 minutes, or until the cheese is melted and starts to brown.

3 Top with the tomato and serve.

SUBSTITUTION TIP Make this recipe with sweet potato chips or vegetable chips if you like. Use the same amount as the tortilla chips and continue with the recipe as indicated.

PER SERVING Calories: 127; Fat: 2g (14% of calories from fat); Saturated Fat: 1g; Protein: 9g; Carbohydrates: 19g; Sodium: 73mg; Fiber: 5g; Sugar: 5g; 29% DV vitamin A; 208% DV vitamin C

Salmon on Bed of Fennel and Carrot, p. 82

FISH AND SEAFOOD

Mustard-Crusted Fish Fillets

PREP 5 minutes / **COOK** 8 to 11 minutes / **SERVES** 4

320°F

Fast

5 teaspoons low-sodium yellow mustard (see Tip)

1 tablespoon freshly squeezed lemon juice

4 (3.5-ounce) sole fillets

½ teaspoon dried thyme

½ teaspoon dried marjoram

⅛ teaspoon freshly ground black pepper

1 slice low-sodium whole-wheat bread, crumbled

2 teaspoons olive oil

AREN'T YOU GLAD YOU DIDN'T DEEP-FRY
The calories from fat dropped by almost half compared to typical fried fish fillets.

Fish fillets turn out wonderfully in the air fryer. The fish stays moist and tender and flakes perfectly at the touch of your fork. And the crispy top, made of low-sodium bread crumbs, herbs, and a bit of olive oil, is the perfect textural contrast to the tender, moist fish.

1 In a small bowl, mix the mustard and lemon juice. Spread this evenly over the fillets. Place them in the air fryer basket.

2 In another small bowl, mix the thyme, marjoram, pepper, bread crumbs, and olive oil. Mix until combined.

3 Gently but firmly press the spice mixture onto the top of each fish fillet.

4 Bake for 8 to 11 minutes, or until the fish reaches an internal temperature of at least 145°F on a meat thermometer and the topping is browned and crisp. Serve immediately.

INGREDIENT TIP Mustard is another ingredient that can be very high in sodium. It's easy to make your own, though: Grind the mustard seeds with water and transfer to a glass jar. Refrigerate for 3 days, stirring twice a day, until you like the way it tastes. You could also add wine or beer to your homemade mustard.

PER SERVING Calories: 142; Fat: 4g (25% of calories from fat); Saturated Fat: 1g; Protein: 20g, Carbohydrates: 5g; Sodium: 140g, Fiber: 1g; Sugar: 1g; 4% DV vitamin C

Fish and Vegetable Tacos

PREP 15 minutes / **COOK** 9 to 12 minutes / **SERVES** 4

390°F

Family Favorite

1 pound white fish fillets, such as sole or cod (see Tip)

2 teaspoons olive oil

3 tablespoons freshly squeezed lemon juice, divided

1½ cups chopped red cabbage

1 large carrot, grated

½ cup low-sodium salsa

⅓ cup low-fat Greek yogurt

4 soft low-sodium whole-wheat tortillas

Tacos are a well-known Tex-Mex street food. They are usually made with refried beans, ground beef, and lots of cheese, sour cream, and guacamole. This lighter version is delicious, with delicate fish and fresh vegetables served in a soft whole-wheat tortilla instead of a fried taco shell.

1 Brush the fish with the olive oil and sprinkle with 1 tablespoon of lemon juice. Air-fry in the air fryer basket for 9 to 12 minutes, or until the fish just flakes when tested with a fork.

2 Meanwhile, in a medium bowl, stir together the remaining 2 tablespoons of lemon juice, the red cabbage, carrot, salsa, and yogurt.

3 When the fish is cooked, remove it from the air fryer basket and break it up into large pieces.

4 Offer the fish, tortillas, and the cabbage mixture, and let each person assemble a taco.

SUBSTITUTION TIP Make these tacos with shrimp instead of fish if you like. Air-fry medium shelled and deveined shrimp for 4 to 6 minutes, until they curl and turn pink. Continue with the recipe as indicated.

PER SERVING Calories: 209; Fat: 3g (13% of calories from fat); Saturated Fat: 0g; Protein: 18g; Carbohydrates: 30g; Sodium: 116mg; Fiber: 1g; Sugar: 4g; 70% DV vitamin A; 43% DV vitamin C

Lighter Fish and Chips

PREP 10 minutes / **COOK** 11 to 15 minutes (chips); 10 to 14 minutes (cod fillets) / **SERVES** 4

390°F

Family Favorite

2 russet potatoes, peeled, thinly sliced, rinsed, and patted dry (see Tip)

1 egg white

1 tablespoon freshly squeezed lemon juice

⅓ cup ground almonds

2 slices low-sodium whole-wheat bread, finely crumbled

½ teaspoon dried basil

4 (4-ounce) cod fillets

AREN'T YOU GLAD YOU DIDN'T DEEP-FRY

Nothing fishy about this—you just cut 25 grams of fat!

Classic battered fish and chips are deep-fried, loaded with sodium, and not a healthy meal. This delicious version is much lighter. Serve with low-sodium tartar sauce if you like.

1 Preheat the oven to warm.

2 Put the potato slices in the air fryer basket and air-fry for 11 to 15 minutes, or until crisp and brown. With tongs, turn the fries twice during cooking.

3 Meanwhile, in a shallow bowl, beat the egg white and lemon juice until frothy.

4 On a plate, mix the almonds, bread crumbs, and basil.

5 One at a time, dip the fillets into the egg white mixture and then into the almond–bread crumb mixture to coat. Place the coated fillets on a wire rack to dry while the fries cook.

6 When the potatoes are done, transfer them to a baking sheet and keep warm in the oven on low heat.

7 Air-fry the fish in the air fryer basket for 10 to 14 minutes, or until the fish reaches an internal temperature of at least 140ºF on a meat thermometer and the coating is browned and crisp. Serve immediately with the potatoes.

INGREDIENT TIP Potato slices cook more quickly than French fries, which is why they are used in this recipe. You can make French fries, which are the classic British "chips," but they need to cook for up to 20 minutes.

PER SERVING Calories: 247; Fat: 5g (18% of calories from fat); Saturated Fat: 0g; Protein: 27g; Carbohydrates: 25g; Sodium: 131mg; Fiber: 3g; Sugar: 3g; 23% DV vitamin C

Snapper with Fruit

PREP 15 minutes / **COOK** 9 to 13 minutes / **SERVES** 4

390°F

Gluten-Free

4 (4-ounce)
red snapper fillets (see Tip)

2 teaspoons olive oil

3 nectarines, halved
and pitted

3 plums, halved and pitted

1 cup red grapes

1 tablespoon freshly
squeezed lemon juice

1 tablespoon honey

½ teaspoon dried thyme

Fruit paired with fish is a tasty treat. The sweet and sour taste of the fruit combines so well with the tender mildness of the red snapper used here. This is a great recipe for a spring dinner—serve with a tossed green salad with mushrooms and drizzle with a simple vinaigrette.

1 Put the red snapper in the air fryer basket and drizzle with the olive oil. Air-fry for 4 minutes.

2 Remove the basket and add the nectarines and plums. Scatter the grapes over all.

3 Drizzle with the lemon juice and honey and sprinkle with the thyme.

4 Return the basket to the air fryer and air-fry for 5 to 9 minutes more, or until the fish flakes when tested with a fork and the fruit is tender. Serve immediately.

SUBSTITUTION TIP Use other mild white fish fillets in place of snapper. Try arctic char, cod, or sole.

PER SERVING Calories: 245; Fat: 4g (15% of calories from fat); Saturated Fat: 1g; Protein: 25g; Carbohydrates: 28g; Sodium: 73mg; Fiber: 3g; Sugar: 24g; 11% DV vitamin A; 27% DV vitamin C

Tuna Wraps

PREP 10 minutes / **COOK** 4 to 7 minutes / **SERVES** 4

390°F

Fast

1 pound fresh tuna steak, cut into 1-inch cubes

1 tablespoon grated fresh ginger

2 garlic cloves, minced

½ teaspoon toasted sesame oil

4 low-sodium whole-wheat tortillas

¼ cup low-fat mayonnaise

2 cups shredded romaine lettuce (see Tip)

1 red bell pepper, thinly sliced

Fresh tuna, cut into chunks and grilled, makes a great wrap when combined with lettuce, red bell pepper, and mayo in a whole-wheat tortilla. This delicious recipe is a nice twist on a simple wrap sandwich.

1 In a medium bowl, mix the tuna, ginger, garlic, and sesame oil. Let it stand for 10 minutes.

2 Grill the tuna in the air fryer for 4 to 7 minutes, or until done to your liking and lightly browned.

3 Make wraps with the tuna, tortillas, mayonnaise, lettuce, and bell pepper. Serve immediately.

PREPARATION TIP To shred lettuce, wash it and pat it dry. Place it on a cutting board and cut across the long leaves with a sharp knife.

PER SERVING Calories: 288; Fat: 7g (22% of calories from fat); Saturated Fat: 2g; Protein: 31g; Carbohydrates: 26g; Sodium: 135mg; Fiber: 1g; Sugar: 1g; 152% DV vitamin A; 36% DV vitamin C

Tuna and Fruit Kebabs

PREP 15 minutes / **COOK** 8 to 12 minutes / **SERVES** 4

370°F

Gluten-Free

1 pound tuna steaks, cut into 1-inch cubes

½ cup canned pineapple chunks, drained, juice reserved

½ cup large red grapes

1 tablespoon honey

2 teaspoons grated fresh ginger

1 teaspoon olive oil

Pinch cayenne pepper

Kebabs, or skewers, make great family meals and are ideal for the air fryer. Bamboo or metal skewers hold tuna and fruit together for easy cooking and serving. The sweet fruit complements the tender seafood, and the honey and pineapple baste adds a touch more sweet flavor.

1 Thread the tuna, pineapple, and grapes on 8 bamboo (see Tip) or 4 metal skewers that fit in the air fryer.

2 In a small bowl, whisk the honey, 1 tablespoon of reserved pineapple juice, the ginger, olive oil, and cayenne. Brush this mixture over the kebabs. Let them stand for 10 minutes.

3 Grill the kebabs for 8 to 12 minutes, or until the tuna reaches an internal temperature of at least 145°F on a meat thermometer, and the fruit is tender and glazed, brushing once with the remaining sauce. Discard any remaining marinade. Serve immediately.

COOKING TIP Soak bamboo skewers in water for 5 or 10 minutes before adding the food so they don't burn as the food cooks.

PER SERVING Calories: 181; Fat: 2g (10% of calories from fat); Saturated Fat: 0g; Protein: 18g; Carbohydrates: 13g; Sodium: 43mg; Fiber: 1g; Sugar: 12g; 3% DV vitamin A; 6% DV vitamin C

Asian Swordfish

PREP 10 minutes / **COOK** 6 to 11 minutes / **SERVES** 4

380°F

Gluten-Free

4 (4-ounce) swordfish steaks

½ teaspoon toasted sesame oil (see Tip)

1 jalapeño pepper, finely minced

2 garlic cloves, grated

1 tablespoon grated fresh ginger

½ teaspoon Chinese five-spice powder

⅛ teaspoon freshly ground black pepper

2 tablespoons freshly squeezed lemon juice

Swordfish steaks are an alternative to salmon and tuna when you want to cook a hearty fish. You may need to order these steaks from the butcher ahead of time, because some grocery stores don't always carry it. The flesh is rich and delicious and is perfectly complemented here with Asian flavors.

1 Place the swordfish steaks on a work surface and drizzle with the sesame oil.

2 In a small bowl, mix the jalapeño, garlic, ginger, five-spice powder, pepper, and lemon juice. Rub this mixture into the fish and let it stand for 10 minutes.

3 Roast the swordfish in the air fryer for 6 to 11 minutes, or until the swordfish reaches an internal temperature of at least 140°F on a meat thermometer. Serve immediately.

INGREDIENT TIP Sesame oil has a wonderfully nutty flavor and is very pungent, so use it sparingly. A small bottle lasts a long time.

PER SERVING Calories: 187; Fat: 6g (29% of calories from fat); Saturated Fat: 1g; Protein: 29g; Carbohydrates: 2g; Sodium: 132mg; Fiber: 0g; Sugar: 1g; 3% DV vitamin A; 15% DV vitamin C

Salmon Spring Rolls

PREP 20 minutes / **COOK** 8 to 10 minutes / **SERVES** 4

370°F

Gluten-Free

½ pound salmon fillet

1 teaspoon toasted sesame oil

1 onion, sliced

8 rice paper wrappers (see Tip)

1 yellow bell pepper, thinly sliced

1 carrot, shredded

⅓ cup chopped fresh flat-leaf parsley

¼ cup chopped fresh basil

This recipe name always makes me think of *Friends*—the episode where Ross tries to teach Rachel and Phoebe about *unagi*, or the state of always being prepared. Rachel responds by saying, "salmon spring roll." Spring rolls are a lighter version of egg rolls with thinner rice paper wrappers and are not usually deep-fried, although you can bake them in the air fryer for some crunch if you like.

1 Put the salmon in the air fryer basket and drizzle with the sesame oil. Add the onion. Air-fry for 8 to 10 minutes, or until the salmon just flakes when tested with a fork and the onion is tender.

2 Meanwhile, fill a small shallow bowl with warm water. One at a time, dip the rice paper wrappers into the water and place on a work surface.

3 Top each wrapper with one-eighth each of the salmon and onion mixture, yellow bell pepper, carrot, parsley, and basil. Roll up the wrapper, folding in the sides, to enclose the ingredients.

4 If you like, bake in the air fryer at 380°F for 7 to 9 minutes, until the rolls are crunchy. Cut the rolls in half to serve.

INGREDIENT TIP Rice paper wrappers are very thin and can tear easily, so handle them with care. They only need to be briefly dipped into the water to soften them enough so you can roll them.

PER SERVING Calories: 95; Fat: 2g (19% of calories from fat); Saturated Fat: 0g; Protein: 13g; Carbohydrates: 8g; Sodium: 98mg; Fiber: 2g; Sugar: 2g; 73% DV vitamin A; 158% DV vitamin C

Salmon on Bed of Fennel and Carrot

PREP 15 minutes / **COOK** 13 to 14 minutes / **SERVES** 2

400°F

Gluten-Free

1 fennel bulb, thinly sliced

1 large carrot, peeled and sliced

1 small onion, thinly sliced

¼ cup low-fat sour cream

¼ teaspoon coarsely ground pepper

2 (5-ounce) salmon fillets

Salmon cooked on a bed of fennel and carrots is a fabulous dish for a special meal. Fennel has a licorice-like flavor that is a great contrast to the sweet carrots and rich and smooth fish.

1 Combine the fennel, carrot, and onion in a bowl and toss.

2 Put the vegetable mixture into a 6-inch metal pan. Roast in the air fryer for 4 minutes or until the vegetables are crisp tender.

3 Remove the pan from the air fryer. Stir in the sour cream and sprinkle the vegetables with the pepper.

4 Top with the salmon fillets.

5 Return the pan to the air fryer. Roast for another 9 to 10 minutes or until the salmon just barely flakes when tested with a fork.

SUBSTITUTION TIP You can use other fish fillets in this easy recipe, but remember that most fillets will cook more quickly than salmon. Orange roughy or halibut fillets will cook in about 5 to 7 minutes.

PER SERVING Calories: 253; Fat 9g (32% calories from fat); Saturated Fat: 1g; Protein: 31g; Carbohydrates: 12g; Sodium: 115mg; Fiber 3g; Sugar: 5g; 130% DV vitamin A; 15% DV vitamin C

Tex-Mex Salmon Stir-Fry

PREP 15 minutes / **COOK** 9 to 14 minutes / **SERVES** 4

370°F

Gluten-Free

12 ounces salmon fillets, cut into 1½-inch cubes (see Tip)

1 red bell pepper, chopped

1 red onion, chopped

1 jalapeño pepper, minced

¼ cup low-sodium salsa

2 tablespoons low-sodium tomato juice

2 teaspoons peanut oil or safflower oil

1 teaspoon chili powder

Brown rice or polenta, cooked (optional)

The air fryer is ideal for cooking stir-fry recipes. You combine all the ingredients in a metal bowl and cook, stirring once during cooking. The Tex-Mex flavors here are a nice change from the typical stir-fry dish. Make this recipe as mild or as spicy as you like.

1 In a medium metal bowl, stir together the salmon, red bell pepper, red onion, jalapeño, salsa, tomato juice, peanut oil, and chili powder.

2 Place the bowl in the air fryer and cook for 9 to 14 minutes, until the salmon is just cooked through and firm and the vegetables are crisp-tender, stirring once. Serve immediately over hot cooked brown rice or polenta, if desired.

INGREDIENT TIP You can use either salmon fillets or salmon steaks for this recipe. The steaks may have some small pin bones; feel for them with your fingers and remove them with tweezers before cooking.

PER SERVING Calories: 116; Fat: 3g (23% of calories from fat); Saturated Fat: 0g; Protein: 18g; Carbohydrates: 5g; Sodium: 136mg; Fiber: 0g; Sugar: 3g; 22% DV vitamin A; 96% DV vitamin C

Scallops with Green Vegetables

PREP 15 minutes / **COOK** 8 to 11 minutes / **SERVES** 4

400°F

Family Favorite, Gluten-Free

1 cup green beans

1 cup frozen peas

1 cup frozen chopped broccoli

2 teaspoons olive oil

½ teaspoon dried basil

½ teaspoon dried oregano

12 ounces sea scallops (see Tip)

If you've never cooked scallops before, you are in for a treat. They are tender and meaty and have the most wonderfully mild flavor. Here they're paired with beautiful bright green vegetables for a visual treat in this simple, satisfying meal.

1 In a large bowl, toss the green beans, peas, and broccoli with the olive oil. Place in the air fryer basket. Air-fry for 4 to 6 minutes, or until the vegetables are crisp-tender.

2 Remove the vegetables from the air fryer basket and sprinkle with the herbs. Set aside.

3 In the air fryer basket, put the scallops and air-fry for 4 to 5 minutes, or until the scallops are firm and reach an internal temperature of just 145ºF on a meat thermometer.

4 Toss scallops with the vegetables and serve immediately.

PREPARATION TIP Sometimes scallops come with a little muscle attached to the side. Pull this off and discard it, as it becomes tough once cooked. That's all the preparation this seafood needs.

PER SERVING Calories: 124; Fat: 3g (22% of calories from fat); Saturated Fat: 0g; Protein: 14g; Carbohydrates: 11g; Sodium: 56mg; Fiber: 3g; Sugar: 3g; 15% DV vitamin A; 46% DV vitamin C

Buttermilk Fried Chicken, p. 99

Six

POULTRY

Roasted Vegetable Chicken Salad

PREP 10 minutes / **COOK** 10 to 13 minutes / **SERVES** 4

400°F

Gluten-Free

3 (4-ounce) low-sodium
boneless skinless chicken
breasts, cut into 1-inch cubes
(see Tip)

1 small red onion, sliced

1 red bell pepper, sliced

1 cup green beans,
cut into 1-inch pieces

2 tablespoons low-fat ranch
salad dressing

2 tablespoons freshly
squeezed lemon juice

½ teaspoon dried basil

4 cups mixed lettuce

This easy-to-make meal is so full of color, flavor, and
nutritional benefits, it's bound to become a regular
on your menu rotation. The chicken and vegetables
cook at the same time and are dressed in a simple
low-fat dressing that adds even more flavor. Dinner
is served!

1 In the air fryer basket, roast the chicken, red onion, red
bell pepper, and green beans for 10 to 13 minutes, or until
the chicken reaches an internal temperature of 165°F on
a meat thermometer, tossing the food in the basket once
during cooking.

2 While the chicken cooks, in a serving bowl, mix the ranch
dressing, lemon juice, and basil.

3 Transfer the chicken and vegetables to a serving bowl
and toss with the dressing to coat. Serve immediately on
lettuce leaves.

INGREDIENT TIP Many brands of boneless skinless chicken
breasts are high in sodium because they are injected with a solution
of salt water to add flavor and increase tenderness. Look at labels
carefully and choose those that have not been "enhanced" this way.

PER SERVING Calories: 113; Fat: 1g (8% of calories from fat); Saturated Fat: 0g;
Protein: 19g; Carbohydrates: 7g; Sodium: 138g; Fiber: 2g; Sugar: 3g; 13% DV
vitamin A; 42% DV vitamin C

Warm Chicken and Spinach Salad

PREP 10 minutes / **COOK** 16 to 20 minutes / **SERVES** 4

400°F

Gluten-Free

3 (5-ounce) low-sodium boneless skinless chicken breasts, cut into 1-inch cubes

5 teaspoons olive oil

½ teaspoon dried thyme

1 medium red onion, sliced

1 red bell pepper, sliced

1 small zucchini, cut into strips

3 tablespoons freshly squeezed lemon juice

6 cups fresh baby spinach (see Tip)

This salad is similar to wilted spinach salads popular in the 1980s, but it is much healthier. There's no bacon, for instance, and the dressing is made from healthy olive oil and lemon juice instead of bacon drippings. Still, this satisfying light lunch or dinner is packed with flavor and is easy to prepare on a busy weeknight.

1 In a large bowl, mix the chicken with the olive oil and thyme. Toss to coat. Transfer to a medium metal bowl and roast for 8 minutes in the air fryer.

2 Add the red onion, red bell pepper, and zucchini. Roast for 8 to 12 minutes more, stirring once during cooking, or until the chicken reaches an internal temperature of 165°F on a meat thermometer.

3 Remove the bowl from the air fryer and stir in the lemon juice.

4 Put the spinach in a serving bowl and top with the chicken mixture. Toss to combine and serve immediately.

SUBSTITUTION TIP You could use other greens in place of the baby spinach. Use a combination of romaine lettuce and kale, or try kale and spinach. Experiment to find the combination you like best.

PER SERVING Calories: 214; Fat: 7g (29% of calories from fat); Saturated Fat: 1g; Protein: 28g; Carbohydrates: 7g; Sodium: 116mg; Fiber: 2g; Sugar: 4g; 90% DV vitamin A; 69% DV vitamin C

Nutty Chicken Nuggets

PREP 10 minutes / **COOK** 10 to 13 minutes / **SERVES** 4

400°F

Family Favorite

1 egg white

1 tablespoon freshly squeezed lemon juice

½ teaspoon dried basil

½ teaspoon ground paprika

1 pound low-sodium boneless skinless chicken breasts, cut into 1½-inch cubes

½ cup ground almonds

2 slices low-sodium whole-wheat bread, crumbled

AREN'T YOU GLAD YOU DIDN'T DEEP-FRY
Air-frying saves 22 grams of fat and 773 milligrams of sodium.

Chicken nuggets are usually made with bread crumbs, which can be high in sodium. Let's add ground almonds for great flavor and some really serious crunch in this childhood favorite. Change the herb used to oregano or thyme if you prefer. Get ready for family fun night!

1 In a shallow bowl, beat the egg white, lemon juice, basil, and paprika with a fork until foamy.

2 Add the chicken and stir to coat.

3 On a plate, mix the almonds and bread crumbs.

4 Toss the chicken cubes in the almond and bread crumb mixture until coated.

5 Bake the nuggets in the air fryer, in two batches, for 10 to 13 minutes, or until the chicken reaches an internal temperature of 165°F on a meat thermometer. Serve immediately.

VARIATION Use the almond and bread crumb mixture to coat whole boneless skinless chicken breasts. Dip the chicken into the egg whites and then into the bread crumbs. Air-fry for about 5 minutes, or until the chicken reaches an internal temperature of 165°F on a meat thermometer.

PER SERVING Calories: 249; Fat: 8g (29% of calories from fat); Saturated Fat: 1g; Protein: 32g; Carbohydrates; 13g; Sodium: 137mg; Fiber: 3g; Sugar: 3g; 3% DV vitamin A; 2% DV vitamin C

Spicy Chicken Meatballs

PREP 10 minutes / **COOK** 11 to 14 minutes / **MAKES** 24 meatballs

400°F

Family Favorite, Gluten-Free

1 medium red onion, minced

2 garlic cloves, minced

1 jalapeño pepper, minced

2 teaspoons olive oil

3 tablespoons
ground almonds

1 egg

1 teaspoon dried thyme

1 pound ground
chicken breast

**AREN'T YOU GLAD
YOU DIDN'T DEEP-FRY**

You saved 135 calories.

Meatballs made with ground chicken are lighter and more tender than the typical meatball made with beef or pork. If you like things spicy, double the jalapeño pepper and add red pepper flakes. Serve these as an appetizer, light lunch, or quick dinner.

1 In a 6-by-2-inch pan, combine the red onion, garlic, jalapeño, and olive oil. Bake for 3 to 4 minutes, or until the vegetables are crisp-tender. Transfer to a medium bowl.

2 Mix in the almonds, egg, and thyme to the vegetable mixture. Add the chicken and mix until just combined.

3 Form the chicken mixture into about 24 (1-inch) balls. Bake the meatballs, in batches, for 8 to 10 minutes, until the chicken reaches an internal temperature of 165°F on a meat thermometer.

SERVING TIP Serve these meatballs in a marinara sauce over hot cooked whole-wheat pasta, or mix them with a stir-fry sauce and serve over rice.

PER SERVING (6 meatballs) Calories: 185; Fat: 7g (34% of calories from fat); Saturated Fat: 1g; Protein: 29g; Carbohydrates: 5g; Sodium: 55mg; Fiber: 1g; Sugar: 3g; 2% DV vitamin A; 10% DV vitamin C

Greek Chicken Kebabs

PREP 15 minutes / **COOK** 15 minutes / **SERVES** 4

380°F

Gluten-Free

3 tablespoons freshly squeezed lemon juice

2 teaspoons olive oil

2 tablespoons chopped fresh flat-leaf parsley

½ teaspoon dried oregano

½ teaspoon dried mint

1 pound low-sodium boneless skinless chicken breasts, cut into 1-inch pieces

1 cup cherry tomatoes

1 small yellow summer squash, cut into 1-inch cubes

Favorite Greek foods include olive oil, lemons, olives, and feta cheese. Unfortunately, two of those ingredients—olives and feta cheese—are very high in sodium. So here we'll use herbs, including oregano, mint, and parsley, to transform ordinary chicken kebabs into a Greek feast.

1 In a large bowl, whisk the lemon juice, olive oil, parsley, oregano, and mint.

2 Add the chicken and stir to coat. Let stand for 10 minutes at room temperature.

3 Alternating the items, thread the chicken, tomatoes, and squash onto 8 bamboo (see Tip, page 79) or metal skewers that fit in an air fryer. Brush with marinade.

4 Grill the kebabs for about 15 minutes, brushing once with any remaining marinade, until the chicken reaches an internal temperature of 165°F on a meat thermometer. Discard any remaining marinade. Serve immediately.

SUBSTITUTION TIP Instead of tomatoes and squash, use other vegetables that will be delicious in this recipe. Try whole button mushrooms; slices of zucchini or red or yellow bell peppers; or onion wedges.

PER SERVING Calories: 163; Fat: 4g (22% of calories from fat); Saturated Fat: 0g; Protein: 27g; Carbohydrates: 4g; Sodium: 70mg; Fiber: 1g; Sugar: 1g; 5% DV vitamin A; 41% DV vitamin C

Tandoori Chicken

PREP 5 minutes, plus marinating time / **COOK** 18 to 23 minutes / **SERVES** 4

360°F

Family Favorite, Gluten-Free

⅔ cup plain low-fat yogurt

2 tablespoons freshly squeezed lemon juice

2 teaspoons curry powder (see Tip)

½ teaspoon ground cinnamon

2 garlic cloves, minced

2 teaspoons olive oil

4 (5-ounce) low-sodium boneless skinless chicken breasts

Tandoori chicken is usually cooked in a tandoori oven, which is a clay oven heated to a very high temperature. The chicken cooks quickly and stays moist and juicy. The air fryer is a great substitute for a tandoori oven, and the results here are subtly spicy and superb.

1 In a medium bowl, whisk the yogurt, lemon juice, curry powder, cinnamon, garlic, and olive oil.

2 With a sharp knife, cut thin slashes into the chicken. Add it to the yogurt mixture and turn to coat. Let stand for 10 minutes at room temperature. You can also prepare this ahead of time and marinate the chicken in the refrigerator for up to 24 hours.

3 Remove the chicken from the marinade and shake off any excess liquid. Discard any remaining marinade.

4 Roast the chicken for 10 minutes. With tongs, carefully turn each piece. Roast for 8 to 13 minutes more, or until the chicken reaches an internal temperature of 165°F on a meat thermometer. Serve immediately.

SUBSTITUTION TIP Substitute any spices you like for the curry powder. Red pepper flakes or cayenne pepper are good if you like spicy food. Or add cumin or allspice.

PER SERVING Calories: 197; Fat: 5g (23% of calories from fat); Saturated Fat: 0g; Protein: 33g; Carbohydrates: 4g; Sodium: 93mg; Fiber: 0g; Sugar: 3g; 6% DV vitamin C

Curried Chicken with Fruit

PREP 12 minutes / **COOK** 18 minutes / **SERVES** 4

380°F

Gluten-Free

3 (5-ounce) low-sodium boneless skinless chicken breasts, cut into 1½-inch cubes (see Tip)

2 teaspoons olive oil

2 tablespoons cornstarch

1 tablespoon curry powder

1 tart apple, chopped

½ cup low-sodium chicken broth

⅓ cup dried cranberries

2 tablespoons freshly squeezed orange juice

Brown rice, cooked (optional)

In India, every family has its own recipe blend of curry powder, which is a combination of turmeric, coriander, cinnamon, chili, and other spices. But the blends found in the grocery store are also good and flavorful. Use your favorite in this simple, fresh recipe.

1 In a medium bowl, mix the chicken and olive oil. Sprinkle with the cornstarch and curry powder. Toss to coat. Stir in the apple and transfer to a 6-by-2-inch metal pan. Bake in the air fryer for 8 minutes, stirring once during cooking.

2 Add the chicken broth, cranberries, and orange juice. Bake for about 10 minutes more, or until the sauce is slightly thickened and the chicken reaches an internal temperature of 165°F on a meat thermometer. Serve over hot cooked brown rice, if desired.

VARIATION Use whole chicken breasts if you like. Increase the cooking time to 20 to 25 minutes, or until the chicken is thoroughly cooked to an internal temperature of 165°F on a meat thermometer.

PER SERVING Calories: 224; Fat: 4g (16% of calories from fat); Saturated Fat: 0g; Protein: 25g; Carbohydrates: 22g; Sodium: 83mg; Fiber: 2g; Sugar: 15g; 1% DV vitamin A; 15% DV vitamin C

Stir-Fried Chicken with Mixed Fruit

PREP 10 minutes / **COOK** 14 to 15 minutes / **SERVES** 4

480°F

Gluten-Free

1 pound low-sodium boneless skinless chicken breasts, cut into 1-inch pieces

1 medium red onion, chopped

1 (8-ounce) can pineapple chunks, drained, ¼ cup juice reserved

1 tablespoon peanut oil or safflower oil

1 peach, peeled, pitted, and cubed

1 tablespoon cornstarch

½ teaspoon ground ginger

¼ teaspoon ground allspice

Brown rice, cooked (optional)

Chicken is the perfect meat to stir-fry. It is tender, flavorful, and easy to cook. Combined with fruit and warm spices in this recipe, this is a nice twist on the classic Asian stir-fry recipe.

1 In a medium metal bowl, mix the chicken, red onion, pineapple, and peanut oil. Cook in the air fryer for 9 minutes. Remove and stir.

2 Add the peach and return the bowl to the air fryer. Cook for 3 minutes more. Remove and stir again.

3 In a small bowl, whisk the reserved pineapple juice, the cornstarch, ginger, and allspice well. Add to the chicken mixture and stir to combine.

4 Cook for 2 to 3 minutes more, or until the chicken reaches an internal temperature of 165°F on a meat thermometer and the sauce is slightly thickened.

5 Serve immediately over hot cooked brown rice, if desired.

PER SERVING Calories: 218; Fat: 5g (21% of calories from fat); Saturated Fat: 1g; Protein: 26g; Carbohydrates: 16g; Sodium: 65mg; Fiber: 1g; Sugar: 11g; 7% DV vitamin C

Tex-Mex Chicken Stir-Fry

PREP 10 minutes / **COOK** 17 to 20 minutes / **SERVES** 4

400°F

Gluten-Free

1 pound low-sodium boneless skinless chicken breasts, cut into 1-inch cubes

1 medium onion, chopped

1 red bell pepper, chopped

1 jalapeño pepper, minced

2 teaspoons olive oil

⅔ cup canned low-sodium black beans, rinsed and drained (see Tip)

½ cup low-sodium salsa

2 teaspoons chili powder

Using the foods and flavors of Tex-Mex cuisine in a stir-fry is a tasty and quick dinner idea. Bell peppers, onion, jalapeño peppers, black beans, and spices pair with tender chicken in this easy recipe. Serve it over hot cooked rice or polenta.

1 In a medium metal bowl, mix the chicken, onion, bell pepper, jalapeño, and olive oil. Stir-fry in the air fryer for 10 minutes, stirring once during cooking.

2 Add the black beans, salsa, and chili powder. Cook for 7 to 10 minutes more, stirring once, until the chicken reaches an internal temperature of 165°F on a meat thermometer. Serve immediately.

INGREDIENT TIP Canned black beans can be very high in sodium; buy those labeled "no salt added." And read the label to make sure the sodium content is low.

PER SERVING Calories: 211; Fat: 4g (17% of calories from fat); Saturated Fat: 0g; Protein: 29g; Carbohydrates: 13g; Sodium: 111mg; Fiber: 4g; Sugar: 4g; 16% DV vitamin A; 36% DV vitamin C

Chicken Fajitas

PREP 15 minutes / **COOK** 10 to 15 minutes / **SERVES** 4

380°F

Family Favorite

4 (5-ounce) low-sodium boneless skinless chicken breasts, cut into 4-by-½-inch strips

1 tablespoon freshly squeezed lemon juice

2 teaspoons olive oil

2 teaspoons chili powder

2 red bell peppers, sliced (see Tip)

4 low-sodium whole-wheat tortillas

⅓ cup nonfat sour cream

1 cup grape tomatoes, sliced (see Tip)

Fajitas are usually made with chicken and vegetables that have been grilled and folded into a soft tortilla with guacamole and sour cream. The air fryer does a great job of grilling these ingredients, with just the right amount of spice for everyone in the family—and you don't have to fuss with a messy charcoal or gas grill!

1 In a large bowl, mix the chicken, lemon juice, olive oil, and chili powder. Toss to coat. Transfer the chicken to the air fryer basket. Add the red bell peppers. Grill for 10 to 15 minutes, or until the chicken reaches an internal temperature of 165°F on a meat thermometer.

2 Assemble the fajitas with the tortillas, chicken, bell peppers, sour cream, and tomatoes. Serve immediately.

SUBSTITUTION TIP Instead of red bell peppers, try zucchini or yellow summer squash cut into strips. And, for a bit more fat (but healthy fat!), use cubed avocado instead of tomatoes.

PER SERVING Calories: 313; Fat: 5g (14% of calories from fat); Saturated Fat: 0g; Protein: 38g; Carbohydrates: 29g; Sodium: 140mg; Fiber: 2g; Sugar: 5g; 23% DV vitamin A; 57% DV vitamin C

Barbecued Chicken

PREP 10 minutes / **COOK** 18 to 20 minutes / **SERVES** 4

370°F

Family Favorite, Gluten-Free

⅓ cup no-salt-added tomato sauce

2 tablespoons low-sodium grainy mustard

2 tablespoons apple cider vinegar

1 tablespoon honey

2 garlic cloves, minced

1 jalapeño pepper, minced

3 tablespoons minced onion

4 (5-ounce) low-sodium boneless skinless chicken breasts (see Tip)

AREN'T YOU GLAD YOU DIDN'T DEEP-FRY
Celebrate 15.5 fewer fat grams and only one-sixth the sodium of a typical fried serving.

Barbecued chicken means summer is here, but it almost always arrives with high levels of sodium and fat. Let's cook boneless skinless chicken breasts in the air fryer with a homemade barbecue sauce that is full of flavor—not fat.

1 In a small bowl, stir together the tomato sauce, mustard, cider vinegar, honey, garlic, jalapeño, and onion.

2 Brush the chicken breasts with some sauce and grill for 10 minutes.

3 Remove the air fryer basket and turn the chicken; brush with more sauce. Grill for 5 minutes more.

4 Remove the air fryer basket and turn the chicken again; brush with more sauce. Grill for 3 to 5 minutes more, or until the chicken reaches an internal temperature of 165°F on a meat thermometer. Discard any remaining sauce. Serve immediately.

SUBSTITUTION TIP Make this recipe with boneless skinless chicken thighs, if you like. The cooking time will be a bit longer, and the finished dish will contain more fat.

PER SERVING Calories: 182; Fat: 2g (10% of calories from fat); Saturated Fat: 0g; Protein: 33g; Carbohydrates: 7g; Sodium: 85mg; Fiber: 1g; Sugar: 5g; 3% DV vitamin A; 10% DV vitamin C

Buttermilk Fried Chicken

PREP 7 minutes / **COOK** 17 to 23 minutes / **SERVES** 4

390°F

Family Favorite

4 (5-ounce) low-sodium boneless skinless chicken breasts, pounded to about ½ inch thick

½ cup buttermilk

½ cup all-purpose flour

2 tablespoons cornstarch

1 teaspoon dried thyme

1 teaspoon ground paprika

1 egg white

1 tablespoon olive oil

AREN'T YOU GLAD YOU DIDN'T DEEP-FRY

With all that crunch, who needs an extra 15 grams of fat and 200 milligrams of sodium at one meal?

Everyone loves fried chicken, but no one loves the fat, sodium, and calories that come along with it! This recipe changes everything. The chicken is moist and tender, and the coating is crunchy and flavorful. Enjoy every crispy, crunchy, flavorful bite.

1 In a shallow bowl, mix the chicken and buttermilk. Let stand for 10 minutes.

2 Meanwhile, in another shallow bowl, mix the flour, cornstarch, thyme, and paprika.

3 In a small bowl, whisk the egg white and olive oil. Quickly stir this egg mixture into the flour mixture so the dry ingredients are evenly moistened.

4 Remove the chicken from the buttermilk and shake off any excess liquid. Dip each piece of chicken into the flour mixture to coat.

5 Air-fry the chicken in the air fryer basket for 17 to 23 minutes, or until the chicken reaches an internal temperature of 165°F on a meat thermometer (see Tip). Serve immediately.

COOKING TIP Cook the chicken in two batches for the crispiest results. Keep the cooked chicken warm in an oven heated to 200°F while the second batch cooks.

PER SERVING Calories: 217; Fat: 6g (29% of calories from fat); Saturated Fat: 1g; Protein: 34g; Carbohydrates: 6g; Sodium: 109mg; Fiber: 0g; Sugar: 1g; 6% DV vitamin A

Chicken with 20 Cloves of Garlic

PREP 5 minutes / **COOK** 25 minutes / **SERVES** 4

370°F

Gluten-Free

4 (5-ounce) low-sodium bone-in skinless chicken breasts (see Tip)

1 tablespoon olive oil

1 tablespoon freshly squeezed lemon juice

3 tablespoons cornstarch

1 teaspoon dried basil leaves

⅛ teaspoon freshly ground black pepper

20 garlic cloves, unpeeled

The famous recipe for chicken with 40 cloves of garlic is delicious but takes a long time to cook. The air fryer speeds up the process, and the result is just as good. The garlic cloves are unpeeled so they steam in their skins. Pinch the garlic out of the skins at the table and eat the soft, sweet cloves with the chicken.

1 Rub the chicken with the olive oil and lemon juice on both sides and sprinkle with the cornstarch, basil, and pepper.

2 Place the seasoned chicken in the air fryer basket and top with the garlic cloves. Roast for about 25 minutes, or until the garlic is soft and the chicken reaches an internal temperature of 165°F on a meat thermometer. Serve immediately.

INGREDIENT TIP You can leave the skin on the chicken while it cooks. It adds a bit of fat to the recipe, but if you remove the skin before you eat the chicken, the additional fat content is minimal.

PER SERVING Calories: 229; Fat: 6g (24% of calories from fat); Saturated Fat: 0g; Protein: 34g; Carbohydrates: 11g; Sodium: 87mg; Fiber: 1g; Sugar: 0g; 13% DV vitamin C

Lemon-Garlic Chicken

PREP 10 minutes / **COOK** 16 to 19 minutes / **SERVES** 4

400°F

Gluten-Free

4 (5-ounce) low-sodium boneless skinless chicken breasts, cut into 4-by-½-inch strips (see Tip)

2 teaspoons olive oil

2 tablespoons cornstarch

3 garlic cloves, minced

½ cup low-sodium chicken broth

¼ cup freshly squeezed lemon juice

1 tablespoon honey

½ teaspoon dried thyme

Brown rice, cooked (optional)

AREN'T YOU GLAD YOU DIDN'T DEEP-FRY

A refreshing reduction of 457 calories, 33 fat grams, and 1,700 milligrams of sodium—in 1 cup.

Lemon and chicken make a perfect pair. The tangy zip of lemon adds flavor to mild chicken, and the acid in the lemon tenderizes the chicken at the same time.

1 In a large bowl, mix the chicken and olive oil. Sprinkle with the cornstarch. Toss to coat.

2 Add the garlic and transfer to a 6-by-2-inch metal pan. Bake in the air fryer for 10 minutes, stirring once during cooking.

3 Add the chicken broth, lemon juice, honey, and thyme to the chicken mixture. Bake for 6 to 9 minutes more, or until the sauce is slightly thickened and the chicken reaches an internal temperature of 165°F on a meat thermometer. Serve over hot cooked brown rice, if desired.

SUBSTITUTION TIP Use boneless skinless chicken thighs for a change of pace. The fat content increases, but, because the fat content in this recipe is so low, it's still a healthy dish. Cook for another 2 to 4 minutes, until the chicken is thoroughly cooked.

PER SERVING Calories: 213; Fat: 4g (17% of calories from fat); Saturated Fat: 0g; Protein: 33g; Carbohydrates: 10g; Sodium: 100mg; Fiber: 0g; Sugar: 5g; 11% DV vitamin C

Mini Turkey Meatloaves

PREP 6 minutes / **COOK** 20 to 24 minutes / **SERVES** 4

400°F

Family Favorite, Gluten-Free

⅓ cup minced onion

¼ cup grated carrot

2 garlic cloves, minced

2 tablespoons
ground almonds

2 teaspoons olive oil

1 teaspoon dried marjoram

1 egg white

¾ pound ground turkey
breast (see Tip)

Mini meatloaves are fun to make and eat. Children, especially, love anything that is kid-size. This flavorful recipe has a lot less fat than a beef meatloaf and is full of good-for-you vegetables. Serve with roasted potatoes and a simple green salad.

1 In a medium bowl, stir together the onion, carrot, garlic, almonds, olive oil, marjoram, and egg white.

2 Add the ground turkey. With your hands, gently but thoroughly mix until combined.

3 Double 16 foil muffin cup liners to make 8 cups. Divide the turkey mixture evenly among the liners.

4 Bake for 20 to 24 minutes, or until the meatloaves reach an internal temperature of 165°F on a meat thermometer. Serve immediately.

SUBSTITUTION TIP Make this recipe with ground chicken breast instead of turkey. Cook the meatloaves until they reach an internal temperature of 165°F on a meat thermometer.

PER SERVING Calories: 141; Fat: 5g (31% of calories from fat); Saturated Fat: 0g; Protein: 23g; Carbohydrates: 3g; Sodium: 61mg; Fiber: 1g; Sugar: 1g; 1% DV vitamin C

Cranberry Turkey Quesadillas

PREP 7 minutes / COOK 4 to 8 minutes / SERVES 4

400°F

Family Favorite, **Fast**

6 low-sodium
whole-wheat tortillas

⅓ cup shredded low-sodium
low-fat Swiss cheese

¾ cup shredded cooked
low-sodium turkey breast

2 tablespoons
cranberry sauce

2 tablespoons dried
cranberries

½ teaspoon dried basil

Olive oil spray, for spraying
the tortillas

This is a great recipe to make with Thanksgiving leftovers, but it's also wonderful any time of year. Cranberry sauce, a bit of cheese, and turkey are grilled with whole-wheat tortillas for a delicious and simple hot sandwich.

1 Put 3 tortillas on a work surface.

2 Evenly divide the Swiss cheese, turkey, cranberry sauce, and dried cranberries among the tortillas. Sprinkle with the basil and top with the remaining tortillas.

3 Spray the outsides of the tortillas with olive oil spray.

4 One at a time, grill the quesadillas in the air fryer for 4 to 8 minutes, or until crisp and the cheese is melted. Cut into quarters and serve.

SUBSTITUTION TIP Quesadillas can be made with almost any leftover. Try crumbled meatloaf, cheese, and grated carrot. Or use leftover sliced pork tenderloin paired with chutney and curry powder.

PER SERVING Calories: 303; Fat: 6g (18% of calories from fat); Saturated Fat: 0g; Protein: 12g; Carbohydrates: 41g; Sodium: 123mg; Fiber: 1g; Sugar: 6g; 1% DV vitamin C

Pork Burgers with Red Cabbage Salad, p. 108

Seven

MEAT

Pork and Mixed Greens Salad

PREP 10 minutes / **COOK** 15 minutes / **SERVES** 4

400°F

Gluten-Free

2 pounds pork tenderloin, cut into 1-inch slices (see Tip)

1 teaspoon olive oil

1 teaspoon dried marjoram

⅛ teaspoon freshly ground black pepper

6 cups mixed salad greens

1 red bell pepper, sliced (see Tip)

1 (8-ounce) package button mushrooms, sliced (see Tip)

⅓ cup low-sodium low-fat vinaigrette dressing

A warm salad for dinner is a nice change of pace. Tender pork is sliced and grilled, then served on a bed of mixed greens with lots of vegetables. Use your favorite salad dressing on this flavorful recipe.

1 In a medium bowl, mix the pork slices and olive oil. Toss to coat.

2 Sprinkle with the marjoram and pepper and rub these into the pork.

3 Grill the pork in the air fryer, in batches, for about 4 to 6 minutes, or until the pork reaches at least 145°F on a meat thermometer.

4 Meanwhile, in a serving bowl, mix the salad greens, red bell pepper, and mushrooms. Toss gently.

5 When the pork is cooked, add the slices to the salad. Drizzle with the vinaigrette and toss gently. Serve immediately.

SUBSTITUTION TIP Substitute sliced chicken or turkey for the pork in this easy salad recipe. Or use different vegetables—sliced zucchini or frozen baby peas are also delicious.

PER SERVING Calories: 172; Fat: 5 g (26% of calories from fat); Saturated Fat: 1g; Protein: 27g; Carbohydrates: 28g; Sodium: 124mg; Fiber: 2g; Sugar: 3g; 63% DV vitamin A; 61% DV vitamin C

Pork Satay

PREP 15 minutes / **COOK** 9 to 14 minutes / **SERVES** 4

380°F

Gluten-Free

1 (1-pound) pork tenderloin, cut into 1½-inch cubes

¼ cup minced onion

2 garlic cloves, minced

1 jalapeño pepper, minced

2 tablespoons freshly squeezed lime juice

2 tablespoons coconut milk

2 tablespoons unsalted peanut butter

2 teaspoons curry powder

Pork satay is a fragrant, rich, mildly spiced Indian recipe that combines pork with onion, garlic, chile, lime juice, coconut milk, spices, and peanut butter. This dish is cooked on skewers and served over rice.

1 In a medium bowl, mix the pork, onion, garlic, jalapeño, lime juice, coconut milk, peanut butter, and curry powder until well combined. Let stand for 10 minutes at room temperature.

2 With a slotted spoon, remove the pork from the marinade. Reserve the marinade.

3 Thread the pork onto about 8 bamboo (see Tip, page 79) or metal skewers. Grill for 9 to 14 minutes, brushing once with the reserved marinade, until the pork reaches at least 145°F on a meat thermometer. Discard any remaining marinade. Serve immediately.

VARIATION Use this marinade on grilled pork chops. Marinate the chops in the mixture for up to 24 hours in the refrigerator. Cook in the air fryer until they reach at least 145°F on a meat thermometer. Always discard any uncooked marinade that has been in contact with raw meat.

PER SERVING Calories: 194; Fat: 7g (32% of calories from fat); Saturated Fat: 3g; Protein: 25g; Carbohydrates: 7g; Sodium: 65mg; Fiber: 1g; Sugar: 3g; 1% DV vitamin A; 11% DV vitamin C

Pork Burgers with Red Cabbage Salad

PREP 20 minutes / **COOK** 7 to 9 minutes / **SERVES** 4

400°F

Family Favorite

½ cup Greek yogurt

2 tablespoons low-sodium mustard, divided

1 tablespoon lemon juice

¼ cup sliced red cabbage

¼ cup grated carrots

1 pound lean ground pork

½ teaspoon paprika

1 cup mixed baby lettuce greens

2 small tomatoes, sliced

8 small low-sodium whole-wheat sandwich buns, cut in half

AREN'T YOU GLAD YOU DIDN'T DEEP-FRY

Deep-fried pork burgers can have almost 80% of their calories from fat.

Have you ever had burgers made with ground pork? They are a bit sweeter and richer than beef burgers. These little burgers, or sliders, are served on whole-wheat buns with a spicy cabbage salad and some fresh tomatoes and greens.

1 In a small bowl, combine the yogurt, 1 tablespoon mustard, lemon juice, cabbage, and carrots; mix and refrigerate.

2 In a medium bowl, combine the pork, remaining 1 tablespoon mustard, and paprika. Form into 8 small patties.

3 Put the sliders into the air fryer basket. Grill for 7 to 9 minutes, or until the sliders register 165°F as tested with a meat thermometer.

4 Assemble the burgers by placing some of the lettuce greens on a bun bottom. Top with a tomato slice, the burgers, and the cabbage mixture. Add the bun top and serve immediately.

RECIPE TIP While whole cuts of pork can be safely eaten if they are cooked to 145°F, ground pork must be cooked to 165°F to kill any bacteria. Always use a meat thermometer to test the doneness of any meat product.

PER SERVING Calories: 472; Fat 15g (29% calories from fat); Saturated Fat: 0g; Protein: 35g; Carbohydrates: 51g; Sodium 138mg; Sugar 8g; Fiber 8g; 11% DV vitamin A; 32% DV vitamin C

Crispy Mustard Pork Tenderloin

PREP 10 minutes / **COOK** 12 to 16 minutes / **SERVES** 4

400°F

3 tablespoons low-sodium grainy mustard

2 teaspoons olive oil

¼ teaspoon dry mustard powder

1 (1-pound) pork tenderloin, silverskin and excess fat trimmed and discarded (see Tip, facing page)

2 slices low-sodium whole-wheat bread, crumbled

¼ cup ground walnuts (see Tip)

2 tablespoons cornstarch

While a definite family favorite, this dish is impressive enough for company. Two kinds of mustard add great flavor to this simple recipe. The coating of bread crumbs, ground walnuts, and cornstarch adds a crispy crust to the tender meat.

1 In a small bowl, stir together the mustard, olive oil, and mustard powder. Spread this mixture over the pork.

2 On a plate, mix the bread crumbs, walnuts, and cornstarch. Dip the mustard-coated pork into the crumb mixture to coat.

3 Air-fry the pork for 12 to 16 minutes, or until it registers at least 145°F on a meat thermometer. Slice to serve.

SUBSTITUTION TIP Other ground nuts are also good in this recipe. Try ground cashews, pecans, or almonds.

PER SERVING Calories: 239; Fat: 9g (34% of calories from fat); Saturated Fat: 2g; Protein: 26g; Carbohydrates: 15g; Sodium: 118mg; Fiber: 2g; Sugar: 3g

Apple Pork Tenderloin

PREP 10 minutes / **COOK** 14 to 19 minutes / **SERVES** 4

400°F

Gluten-Free

1 (1-pound) pork tenderloin, cut into 4 pieces (see Tip)

1 tablespoon apple butter

2 teaspoons olive oil

2 Granny Smith apples or Jonagold apples, sliced

3 celery stalks, sliced

1 onion, sliced

½ teaspoon dried marjoram

⅓ cup apple juice

Apples and pork combine to make an excellent fall-themed dinner. Onions and celery add more flavor and nutrition. Serve with a green salad with mushrooms and a glass of white wine.

1 Rub each piece of pork with the apple butter and olive oil.

2 In a medium metal bowl, mix the pork, apples, celery, onion, marjoram, and apple juice.

3 Place the bowl into the air fryer and roast for 14 to 19 minutes, or until the pork reaches at least 145°F on a meat thermometer and the apples and vegetables are tender. Stir once during cooking. Serve immediately.

SUBSTITUTION TIP Make this recipe with chicken breasts instead of pork if you like. Cut each chicken breast in half crosswise to use in the recipe. Cook the chicken until it reaches 165°F on a meat thermometer.

PER SERVING Calories: 213; Fat: 5g (21% of calories from fat); Saturated Fat: 1g; Protein: 24g; Carbohydrates: 20g; Sodium: 88mg; Fiber: 3g; Sugar: 15g; 4% DV vitamin A; 26% DV vitamin C

Espresso-Grilled Pork Tenderloin

PREP 15 minutes / **COOK** 9 to 11 minutes / **SERVES** 4

400°F

Gluten-Free

1 tablespoon packed brown sugar

2 teaspoons espresso powder

1 teaspoon ground paprika

½ teaspoon dried marjoram

1 tablespoon honey

1 tablespoon freshly squeezed lemon juice

2 teaspoons olive oil

1 (1-pound) pork tenderloin

Espresso powder is concentrated instant coffee that adds a rich, smoky flavor to meat. Pork tenderloin has very little fat and is a naturally tender cut. Combine the two, along with some spices, for an entrée that perks up any dinner!

1 In a small bowl, mix the brown sugar, espresso powder, paprika, and marjoram.

2 Stir in the honey, lemon juice, and olive oil until well mixed.

3 Spread the honey mixture over the pork and let stand for 10 minutes at room temperature.

4 Roast the tenderloin in the air fryer basket for 9 to 11 minutes, or until the pork registers at least 145°F on a meat thermometer. Slice the meat to serve.

VARIATION Use this rub on other cuts of pork, too, such as pork chops or pork cubes cut from the shoulder or loin.

PER SERVING Calories: 177; Fat: 5g (25% of calories from fat); Saturated Fat: 1g; Protein: 23g; Carbohydrates: 10g; Sodium: 61mg; Fiber: 1g; Sugar: 8g; 6% DV vitamin A; 3% DV vitamin C

Pork and Potatoes

PREP 5 minutes / **COOK** 25 minutes / **SERVES** 4

370°F

Gluten-Free

2 cups creamer potatoes, rinsed and dried (see Tip)

2 teaspoons olive oil

1 (1-pound) pork tenderloin, cut into 1-inch cubes

1 onion, chopped

1 red bell pepper, chopped

2 garlic cloves, minced

½ teaspoon dried oregano

2 tablespoons low-sodium chicken broth

Creamer potatoes are very young Yukon Gold or red potatoes, harvested before they mature. They are about 1 inch in diameter and are very tender, with a creamy texture. They pair beautifully with pork in this simple one-dish dinner.

1 In a medium bowl, toss the potatoes and olive oil to coat.

2 Transfer the potatoes to the air fryer basket. Roast for 15 minutes.

3 In a medium metal bowl, mix the potatoes, pork, onion, red bell pepper, garlic, and oregano.

4 Drizzle with the chicken broth. Put the bowl in the air fryer basket. Roast for about 10 minutes more, shaking the basket once during cooking, until the pork reaches at least 145°F on a meat thermometer and the potatoes are tender. Serve immediately.

SUBSTITUTION TIP If you can't find creamer potatoes, any small potato will do. If the potatoes are larger than 1 inch in diameter, cut them into pieces or slices so they cook in the designated time.

PER SERVING Calories: 235; Fat: 5g (19% of calories from fat); Saturated Fat: 1g; Protein: 26g; Carbohydrates: 22g; Sodium: 66mg; Fiber: 3g; Sugar: 4g; 8% DV vitamin A; 36% DV vitamin C

Pork and Fruit Kebabs

PREP 15 minutes / **COOK** 9 to 12 minutes / **SERVES** 4

380°F

Family Favorite, Gluten-Free

⅓ cup apricot jam

2 tablespoons freshly squeezed lemon juice

2 teaspoons olive oil

½ teaspoon dried tarragon

1 (1-pound) pork tenderloin, cut into 1-inch cubes

4 plums, pitted and quartered (see Tip)

4 small apricots, pitted and halved (see Tip)

Kebabs are easy and quick to grill in the air fryer. And pork is a great choice for kebabs. This recipe uses fresh plums and apricots for added flavor and nutrition. Cook the pork to a minimum temperature of 145°F for food safety reasons.

1 In a large bowl, mix the jam, lemon juice, olive oil, and tarragon.

2 Add the pork and stir to coat. Let stand for 10 minutes at room temperature.

3 Alternating the items, thread the pork, plums, and apricots onto 4 metal skewers that fit into the air fryer. Brush with any remaining jam mixture. Discard any remaining marinade.

4 Grill the kebabs in the air fryer for 9 to 12 minutes, or until the pork reaches 145°F on a meat thermometer and the fruit is tender. Serve immediately.

SUBSTITUTION TIP Other stone fruits are also delicious in this recipe. Try sliced peaches or use small nectarines that have been halved. Large grapes are also good.

PER SERVING Calories: 256; Fat; 5g (17% of calories from fat); Saturated Fat; 1g; Protein: 24g; Carbohydrates: 30g; Sodium: 60mg; Fiber: 2g; Sugar: 22g; 24% DV vitamin A; 29% DV vitamin C

Steak and Vegetable Kebabs

PREP 15 minutes / **COOK** 5 to 7 minutes / **SERVES** 4

390°F

Family Favorite, Gluten-Free

2 tablespoons
balsamic vinegar

2 teaspoons olive oil

½ teaspoon dried marjoram

⅛ teaspoon freshly ground
black pepper

¾ pound round steak,
cut into 1-inch pieces

1 red bell pepper, sliced
(see Tip)

16 button mushrooms
(see Tip)

1 cup cherry tomatoes
(see Tip)

Colorful vegetables make this meal delicious and very healthy. Italian balsamic vinegar, aged in wooden casks to add flavor and color, adds a wonderful depth of flavor to these kebabs. Trim visible fat from the steak before you thread the cubes onto the skewers.

1 In a medium bowl, stir together the balsamic vinegar, olive oil, marjoram, and black pepper.

2 Add the steak and stir to coat. Let stand for 10 minutes at room temperature.

3 Alternating items, thread the beef, red bell pepper, mushrooms, and tomatoes onto 8 bamboo (see Tip, page 79) or metal skewers that fit in the air fryer.

4 Grill in the air fryer for 5 to 7 minutes, or until the beef is browned and reaches at least 145°F on a meat thermometer. Serve immediately.

SUBSTITUTION TIP Use other vegetables in this versatile recipe. Onion wedges grill very well, as do zucchini or yellow summer squash slices.

PER SERVING Calories: 194; Fat: 6g (28% of calories from fat); Saturated Fat: 2g; Protein: 31g; Carbohydrates: 7g; Sodium: 53mg; Fiber: 2g; Sugar: 2g; 9% DV vitamin A; 35% DV vitamin C

Spicy Grilled Steak

PREP 7 minutes / **COOK** 6 to 9 minutes / **SERVES** 4

390°F

Fast, Gluten-Free

2 tablespoons
low-sodium salsa

1 tablespoon minced
chipotle pepper

1 tablespoon apple
cider vinegar

1 teaspoon ground cumin

⅛ teaspoon freshly ground
black pepper

⅛ teaspoon red pepper flakes

¾ pound sirloin tip steak,
cut into 4 pieces and
gently pounded to
about ⅓ inch thick (see Tip)

This spicy steak gets its kick from chipotle peppers and red pepper flakes. It's very simple to make and delicious served with salsa, guacamole, and pita breads or naan.

1 In a small bowl, thoroughly mix the salsa, chipotle pepper, cider vinegar, cumin, black pepper, and red pepper flakes. Rub this mixture into both sides of each steak piece. Let stand for 15 minutes at room temperature.

2 Grill the steaks in the air fryer, two at a time, for 6 to 9 minutes, or until they reach at least 145°F on a meat thermometer.

3 Remove the steaks to a clean plate and cover with aluminum foil to keep warm. Repeat with the remaining steaks.

4 Slice the steaks thinly against the grain and serve.

INGREDIENT TIP Always read labels when you buy steaks. The leanest cuts of beef include sirloin tip steak, top round steak, and top sirloin steak.

PER SERVING Calories: 160; Fat: 6g (33% of calories from fat); Saturated Fat: 3g; Protein: 24g; Carbohydrates: 1g; Sodium: 87mg; Fiber: 0g; Sugar: 0g; 2% DV vitamin A

Greek Vegetable Skillet

PREP 10 minutes / **COOK** 9 to 19 minutes / **SERVES** 4

370°F

Gluten-Free

½ pound 96-percent lean ground beef

2 medium tomatoes, chopped

1 onion, chopped

2 garlic cloves, minced

2 cups fresh baby spinach (see Tip)

2 tablespoons freshly squeezed lemon juice

⅓ cup low-sodium beef broth

2 tablespoons crumbled low-sodium feta cheese

The flavors of Greece combine in this easy one-dish meal, made with lean ground beef, spinach, and tomatoes. A bit of feta cheese is added for flavor, but not enough to increase the sodium content much.

1 In a 6-by-2-inch metal pan, crumble the beef. Cook in the air fryer for 3 to 7 minutes, stirring once during cooking, until browned. Drain off any fat or liquid.

2 Add the tomatoes, onion, and garlic to the pan. Air-fry for 4 to 8 minutes more, or until the onion is tender.

3 Add the spinach, lemon juice, and beef broth. Air-fry for 2 to 4 minutes more, or until the spinach is wilted.

4 Sprinkle with the feta cheese and serve immediately.

SUBSTITUTION TIP Substitute other vegetables, such as chopped zucchini or sliced mushrooms, for the spinach in this recipe, if you prefer.

PER SERVING Calories: 97; Fat: 1g (10% of calories from fat); Saturated Fat: 1g; Protein: 15g; Carbohydrates: 5g; Sodium: 123mg; Fiber: 1g; Sugar: 2g; 35% DV vitamin A; 28% DV vitamin C

Light Herbed Meatballs

PREP 10 minutes / **COOK** 12 to 17 minutes / **MAKES** 24 meatballs

380°F

1 medium onion, minced

2 garlic cloves, minced

1 teaspoon olive oil

1 slice low-sodium whole-wheat bread, crumbled

3 tablespoons 1 percent milk

1 teaspoon dried marjoram

1 teaspoon dried basil

1 pound 96-percent lean ground beef

AREN'T YOU GLAD YOU DIDN'T DEEP-FRY

Definitely not light—deep-frying means you almost double your calories from fat.

Using extra-lean ground beef really trims the fat in these meatballs. But lean beef can be tough, so we add bread crumbs and milk to keep them tender. Dried herbs add flavor.

1 In a 6-by-2-inch pan, combine the onion, garlic, and olive oil. Air-fry for 2 to 4 minutes, or until the vegetables are crisp-tender.

2 Transfer the vegetables to a medium bowl, and add the bread crumbs, milk, marjoram, and basil. Mix well.

3 Add the ground beef. With your hands, work the mixture gently but thoroughly until combined. Form the meat mixture into about 24 (1-inch) meatballs.

4 Bake the meatballs, in batches, in the air fryer basket for 12 to 17 minutes, or until they reach 160°F on a meat thermometer. Serve immediately.

SERVING TIP Use these meatballs to make everybody's favorite: spaghetti and meatballs. Add them to jarred marinara sauce and serve over hot cooked whole-grain spaghetti. They also make a tasty meatball sub.

PER SERVING (6 meatballs) Calories: 190; Fat: 6g (28% of calories from fat); Saturated Fat: 2g; Protein: 25g; Carbohydrates: 8g; Sodium: 120mg; Fiber: 1g; Sugar: 2g; 1% DV vitamin A; 3% DV vitamin C

Brown Rice and Beef-Stuffed Bell Peppers

PREP 10 minutes / **COOK** 11 to 16 minutes / **SERVES** 4

400°F

Gluten-Free

4 medium bell peppers, any colors, rinsed, tops removed

1 medium onion, chopped

½ cup grated carrot

2 teaspoons olive oil

2 medium beefsteak tomatoes, chopped

1 cup cooked brown rice

1 cup chopped cooked low-sodium roast beef (see Tip)

1 teaspoon dried marjoram

Stuffed bell peppers are a trusty old-fashioned recipe that is delicious and can be healthy, too. Just a bit of leftover roast beef adds flavor but without too much fat. Use different colored peppers for a fun presentation.

1 Remove the stems from the bell pepper tops and chop the tops.

2 In a 6-by-2-inch pan, combine the chopped bell pepper tops, onion, carrot, and olive oil. Cook for 2 to 4 minutes, or until the vegetables are crisp-tender.

3 Transfer the vegetables to a medium bowl. Add the tomatoes, brown rice, roast beef, and marjoram. Stir to mix.

4 Stuff the vegetable mixture into the bell peppers. Place the bell peppers in the air fryer basket. Bake for 11 to 16 minutes, or until the peppers are tender and the filling is hot. Serve immediately.

SUBSTITUTION TIP Use any cooked meat you like in this easy recipe, such as pork tenderloin or chicken thighs. You could also add more vegetables, minced garlic cloves, or chopped zucchini.

PER SERVING Calories: 206; Fat: 6g (26% of calories from fat); Saturated Fat: 1g; Protein: 18g; Carbohydrates: 20g; Sodium: 105mg; Fiber: 3g; Sugar: 5g; 41% DV vitamin A; 138% DV vitamin C

Beef and Broccoli

PREP 10 minutes / COOK 14 to 18 minutes / SERVES 4

400°F

Family Favorite, Gluten-Free

2 tablespoons cornstarch

½ cup low-sodium beef broth

1 teaspoon low-sodium soy sauce

12 ounces sirloin strip steak, cut into 1-inch cubes

2½ cups broccoli florets

1 onion, chopped

1 cup sliced cremini mushrooms (see Tip)

1 tablespoon grated fresh ginger

Brown rice, cooked (optional)

Beef and broccoli is a familiar Chinese dish that is usually made with lots of soy sauce and oyster sauce, which sends the sodium content through the roof. Mushrooms are used instead in this easy recipe because they add a meaty flavor that is a good substitute for those high-sodium ingredients.

1 In a medium bowl, stir together the cornstarch, beef broth, and soy sauce.

2 Add the beef and toss to coat. Let stand for 5 minutes at room temperature.

3 With a slotted spoon, transfer the beef from the broth mixture into a medium metal bowl. Reserve the broth.

4 Add the broccoli, onion, mushrooms, and ginger to the beef. Place the bowl into the air fryer and cook for 12 to 15 minutes, or until the beef reaches at least 145°F on a meat thermometer and the vegetables are tender.

5 Add the reserved broth and cook for 2 to 3 minutes more, or until the sauce boils.

6 Serve immediately over hot cooked brown rice, if desired.

INGREDIENT TIP Cremini mushrooms are baby portobello mushrooms. They are brown in color and have more flavor than button mushrooms. Substitute button mushrooms if you can't find the cremini variety.

PER SERVING Calories: 240; Fat: 6g (23% of calories from fat); Saturated Fat: 2g; Protein: 19g; Carbohydrates: 11g; Sodium: 107mg; Fiber: 2g; Sugar: 3g; 49% DV vitamin C

Beef and Fruit Stir-Fry

PREP 15 minutes / COOK 6 to 11 minutes / SERVES 4

370°F

Gluten-Free

12 ounces sirloin tip steak, thinly sliced

1 tablespoon freshly squeezed lime juice

1 cup canned mandarin orange segments, drained, juice reserved (see Tip)

1 cup canned pineapple chunks, drained, juice reserved (see Tip)

1 teaspoon low-sodium soy sauce

1 tablespoon cornstarch

1 teaspoon olive oil

2 scallions, white and green parts, sliced

Brown rice, cooked (optional)

Meaty, tender beef is delicious paired with the sweet and tart flavors of fruit, but this recipe isn't very common. Don't let that keep you from trying this dish. Serve over hot cooked rice or polenta that has been cooled, sliced, and grilled in the air fryer.

1 In a medium bowl, mix the steak with the lime juice. Set aside.

2 In a small bowl, thoroughly mix 3 tablespoons of reserved mandarin orange juice, 3 tablespoons of reserved pineapple juice, the soy sauce, and cornstarch.

3 Drain the beef and transfer it to a medium metal bowl, reserving the juice. Stir the reserved juice into the mandarin-pineapple juice mixture. Set aside.

4 Add the olive oil and scallions to the steak. Place the metal bowl in the air fryer and cook for 3 to 4 minutes, or until the steak is almost cooked, shaking the basket once during cooking.

5 Stir in the mandarin oranges, pineapple, and juice mixture. Cook for 3 to 7 minutes more, or until the sauce is bubbling and the beef is tender and reaches at least 145°F on a meat thermometer.

6 Stir and serve over hot cooked brown rice, if desired.

SUBSTITUTION TIP Other fruits can be used in this recipe. Try cubed apples, pears, or even peaches and grapes. You could also add herbs—dried thyme or marjoram would be delicious.

PER SERVING Calories: 212; Fat: 4g (17% of calories from fat); Saturated Fat: 1g; Protein: 19g; Carbohydrates: 28g; Sodium: 105mg; Fiber: 2g; Sugar: 22g; 14% DV vitamin A; 46% DV vitamin C

Beef Risotto

PREP 6 minutes / **COOK** 20 to 24 minutes / **SERVES** 4

390°F

Gluten-Free

2 teaspoons olive oil

1 onion, finely chopped

3 garlic cloves, minced

½ cup chopped red bell pepper

¾ cup short-grain rice

1¼ cups low-sodium beef broth

½ cup (about 3 ounces) chopped cooked roast beef (see Tip)

3 tablespoons grated Parmesan cheese

Risotto is simply a combination of short-grain rice and broth that is cooked and stirred constantly on the stove top until creamy. This version of the classic Italian dish is made in your air fryer with much less work. The vegetables add color, texture, and nutritional value.

1 In a 6-by-2-inch pan, combine the olive oil, onion, garlic, and red bell pepper. Place the pan in the air fryer for 2 minutes, or until the vegetables are crisp-tender. Remove from the air fryer.

2 Add the rice, beef broth, and roast beef. Return the pan to the air fryer and bake for 18 to 22 minutes, stirring once during cooking, until the rice is tender and the beef reaches at least 145°F on a meat thermometer. Remove the pan from the air fryer.

3 Stir in the Parmesan cheese and serve immediately.

INGREDIENT TIP In most large supermarkets, you can often find roast beef at the deli. It can be high in sodium, so ask about its nutrition before you buy.

PER SERVING Calories: 227; Fat: 5g (20% of calories from fat); Saturated Fat: 2g; Protein: 10g; Carbohydrates: 33g, Sodium: 88mg; Fiber: 2g; Sugar: 2g; 12% DV vitamin A; 62% DV vitamin C

Brown Rice Fritters, p. 132

Eight

VEGETABLES AND SIDES

Herb-Roasted Vegetables

PREP 10 minutes / **COOK** 14 to 18 minutes / **SERVES** 4

350°F

Gluten-Free, Vegan,
Very Low Sodium

1 red bell pepper, sliced

1 (8-ounce) package sliced mushrooms

1 cup green beans, cut into 2-inch pieces

⅓ cup diced red onion

3 garlic cloves, sliced

1 teaspoon olive oil (see Tip)

½ teaspoon dried basil

½ teaspoon dried tarragon

Roasted vegetables make a colorful, nutrient-filled side dish for any entrée, from roasted chicken to grilled fish. This recipe uses tender vegetables. Substitute your favorite herbs, if you prefer, in the same amounts.

1 In a medium bowl, mix the red bell pepper, mushrooms, green beans, red onion, and garlic. Drizzle with the olive oil. Toss to coat.

2 Add the herbs and toss again.

3 Place the vegetables in the air fryer basket. Roast for 14 to 18 minutes, or until tender. Serve immediately.

SUBSTITUTION TIP Some oil is necessary in this recipe so the dried herbs stick to the vegetables as they roast and do not float around inside the cooker. You can use cooking spray instead to cut the fat.

PER SERVING Calories: 41; Fat: 1g (20% of calories from fat); Saturated Fat: 0g; Protein: 2g; Carbohydrates: 5g; Sodium: 9mg; Fiber: 2g; Sugar: 3g; 12% DV vitamin A; 32% DV vitamin C

Crispy Broccoli

PREP 10 minutes / **COOK** 11 minutes / **SERVES** 4

380°F

Gluten-Free, Vegan

1 large head fresh broccoli
2 teaspoons olive oil
1 tablespoon lemon juice

AREN'T YOU GLAD YOU DIDN'T DEEP-FRY

Deep-fried broccoli can have as much as 44% calories from fat.

When broccoli is roasted, it becomes sweet and slightly crisp around the edges. This super easy and healthy recipe will make broccoli lovers out of everyone! This makes an excellent side dish, or you can even serve it as an appetizer with a dip made from yogurt and salsa.

1 Rinse the broccoli and pat dry. Cut off the florets and separate them. You can use the stems of the broccoli too; cut them into 1" chunks and peel them.

2 Toss the broccoli, olive oil, and lemon juice in a large bowl until coated.

3 Roast the broccoli, in batches, for 10 to 14 minutes or until the broccoli is crisp-tender and slightly brown around the edges. Repeat with the remaining broccoli. Serve immediately.

INGREDIENT TIP You can cook cauliflower using this method too! Just rinse it, cut into florets, toss with the olive oil and lemon juice, and roast. It's delicious as a side dish or an appetizer.

PER SERVING Calories: 63; Fat: 2g (29% of calories from fat); Saturated Fat: 0g; Protein: 4g; Carbohydrates: 10g; Sodium: 50mg; Fiber: 4g; Sugar: 3g; 19% DV vitamin A; 228% DV vitamin C

Garlic-Roasted Bell Peppers

PREP 10 minutes / **COOK** 18 to 20 minutes / **SERVES** 4

350°F

Gluten-Free, Vegan,
Very Low Sodium

4 bell peppers, any colors, stemmed, seeded, membranes removed, and cut into fourths

1 teaspoon olive oil

4 garlic cloves, minced

½ teaspoon dried thyme

Roasted bell peppers can be used for so many things. When drizzled with balsamic vinegar and olive oil, they make a wonderful appetizer for an antipasto platter. They are delicious in fajitas and can be used in many Tex-Mex recipes. But they are best seasoned with garlic and served as a simple side dish.

1 Place the peppers into the air fryer basket and drizzle with the olive oil. Toss gently. Roast for 15 minutes.

2 Sprinkle with the garlic and thyme. Roast for 3 to 5 minutes more, or until tender (see Tip). Serve immediately.

COOKING TIP You can peel the bell peppers after they are cooked if you like. To do that, put the hot peppers into a food-safe paper bag, close it, and steam for 2 to 4 minutes. The skins peel right off.

PER SERVING Calories: 36; Fat: 1g (25% of calories from fat); Saturated Fat: 0g; Protein: 1g; Carbohydrates: 5g; Sodium: 21mg; Fiber: 2g; Sugar: 3g; 18% DV vitamin A; 148% DV vitamin C

Curried Brussels Sprouts

PREP 13 minutes / **COOK** 15 to 17 minutes / **SERVES** 4

390°F

Gluten-Free, Vegan,
Very Low Sodium

1 pound Brussels sprouts, ends trimmed, discolored leaves removed, halved lengthwise

2 teaspoons olive oil

3 teaspoons curry powder, divided

1 tablespoon freshly squeezed lemon juice

Brussels sprouts are famous for being hated, especially by children. These little cabbages can be bitter, but not when roasted until crisp on the outside and tender on the inside, and mildly flavored with curry powder. Try this dish as an accompaniment to roasted chicken.

1 In a large bowl, toss the Brussels sprouts with the olive oil and 1 teaspoon of curry powder. Transfer to the air fryer basket. Roast for 12 minutes, shaking the basket once during cooking.

2 Sprinkle with the remaining 2 teaspoons of the curry powder and the lemon juice. Shake again. Roast for 3 to 5 minutes more, or until the Brussels sprouts are browned and crisp (see Tip). Serve immediately.

COOKING TIP To test the Brussels sprouts for doneness, try to pierce one with a toothpick. The toothpick should slide easily into the little sprout, while the outside will be caramelized.

PER SERVING Calories: 86; Fat: 3g (31% of calories from fat); Saturated Fat: 0g; Protein: 4g; Carbohydrates: 12g; Sodium: 21mg; Fiber: 4g; Sugar: 3g; 5% DV vitamin A; 123% DV vitamin C

Asparagus with Garlic

PREP 5 minutes / **COOK** 4 to 5 minutes, or 8 to 11 minutes depending on desired texture / **SERVES** 4

380°F

Fast, Gluten-Free, Vegan

1 pound asparagus, rinsed, ends snapped off where they naturally break (see Tip)

2 teaspoons olive oil

3 garlic cloves, minced

2 tablespoons balsamic vinegar

½ teaspoon dried thyme

Asparagus cooks perfectly in the air fryer. You have a choice in the end result: tender with a bit of a bite or roasted until crisp and brown on the outside and tender on the inside. Garlic adds a slightly zippy finishing touch.

1 In a large bowl, toss the asparagus with the olive oil. Transfer to the air fryer basket.

2 Sprinkle with garlic. Roast for 4 to 5 minutes for crisp-tender or for 8 to 11 minutes for asparagus that is crisp on the outside and tender on the inside.

3 Drizzle with the balsamic vinegar and sprinkle with the thyme leaves. Serve immediately.

INGREDIENT TIP It doesn't matter whether you buy thin or thick asparagus spears; they will be tender if cooked properly. The thicker spears, obviously, take a bit more time to cook.

PER SERVING Calories: 41; Fat: 1g (22% of calories from fat); Saturated Fat: 0g; Protein: 3g; Carbohydrates: 6g; Sodium: 3mg; Fiber: 2g; Sugar: 3g; 17% DV vitamin A; 12% DV vitamin C

Glazed Carrots and Sweet Potatoes

PREP 5 minutes / **COOK** 20 to 25 minutes / **SERVES** 4

400°F

Gluten-Free, Vegetarian

2 large carrots,
cut into chunks

1 medium sweet potato,
peeled and cut into
1-inch cubes

½ cup chopped onion

2 garlic cloves, minced

2 tablespoons honey

1 tablespoon freshly
squeezed orange juice

2 teaspoons butter, melted

Carrots and sweet potatoes are two of the healthiest vegetables you can eat. They are packed with fiber and lots of vitamin A. And they taste delicious, especially when roasted, which caramelizes the sugars in these root vegetables. Orange juice keeps the vegetables tender and adds bright flavor to this easy side dish.

1 In a 6-by-2-inch pan, toss the carrots, sweet potato, onion, garlic, honey, orange juice, and butter to coat.

2 Roast for 15 minutes. Check the vegetables. Shake the basket and roast for 5 to 10 minutes more, or until the vegetables are tender and glazed. Serve immediately.

INGREDIENT NOTE The sweet potatoes you buy in the supermarket are not yams. Yams are drier and starchier, usually with a white-colored flesh and not as sweet as sweet potatoes.

PER SERVING Calories: 105; Fat: 2g (17% of calories from fat); Saturated Fat: 1g; Protein: 1g; Carbohydrates: 21g; Sodium: 59mg; Fiber: 2g; Sugar: 13g; 216% DV vitamin A; 11% DV vitamin C

Scalloped Mixed Vegetables

PREP 10 minutes / **COOK** 20 minutes / **SERVES** 4

380°F

Gluten-Free, Vegetarian

1 Yukon Gold potato, thinly sliced

1 small sweet potato, peeled and thinly sliced

1 medium carrot, thinly sliced

¼ cup minced onion

3 garlic cloves, minced

¾ cup 2 percent milk

2 tablespoons cornstarch

½ teaspoon dried thyme

Scalloped potatoes are the ultimate comfort food, but there is not much comfort in the fact that they aren't very good for you. So let's increase the nutritional benefits with other root vegetables that are high in vitamin A and lower-fat products. This is a great dish to serve with roast chicken or pork loin for a winter dinner.

1 In a 6-by-2-inch pan, layer the potato, sweet potato, carrot, onion, and garlic.

2 In a small bowl, whisk the milk, cornstarch, and thyme until blended. Pour the milk mixture evenly over the vegetables in the pan.

3 Bake for 15 minutes. Check the casserole—it should be golden brown on top, and the vegetables should be tender. If they aren't, bake for 4 to 5 minutes more. Serve immediately.

VARIATION Top these potatoes with cheese after about 10 minutes of baking if you like. Add ¼ cup shredded low-fat mozzarella or Swiss cheese and bake until the cheese is bubbling and starts to brown. Remember, this increases the fat and sodium content.

PER SERVING Calories: 95; Fat: 1g (9% of calories from fat); Saturated Fat: 1g; Protein: 3g; Carbohydrates: 19g; Sodium: 49mg; Fiber: 2g; Sugar: 5g; 147% DV vitamin A; 9% DV vitamin C

Crispy Sweet Potato Wedges

PREP 5 minutes / **COOK** 20 to 25 minutes / **SERVES** 4

400°F

Family Favorite,
Gluten-Free, Vegan

2 sweet potatoes, peeled and cut into ½-inch wedges

2 teaspoons olive oil

2 tablespoons cornstarch

1 teaspoon ground cinnamon

¼ teaspoon ground allspice

¼ teaspoon ground nutmeg

⅛ teaspoon cayenne pepper

AREN'T YOU GLAD YOU <u>DIDN'T</u> DEEP-FRY

Air-frying cuts 120 calories—more than half per serving.

Sweet potatoes, when cooked in the air fryer, are light and crisp on the outside and tender and velvety on the inside. This recipe is seasoned with cinnamon, nutmeg, allspice, and cayenne pepper for sweet and heat. Serve them as a side dish to a pot roast or roasted chicken for a great meal.

1 In a medium bowl of warm water, soak the sweet potato wedges for 10 minutes. Drain and pat dry with paper towels. Toss with the olive oil.

2 Put half the potato wedges into the air fryer basket and roast for 8 minutes. Transfer the fries to a large bowl (see Tip). Repeat with the remaining sweet potato wedges.

3 In the large bowl, sprinkle all the potatoes with the cornstarch and toss very thoroughly to coat; this should take at least 2 minutes.

4 Sprinkle with the cinnamon, allspice, nutmeg, and cayenne. Toss again.

5 Return half the wedges to the air fryer and roast for 12 to 17 minutes more, until the potatoes are golden brown and crisp, tossing the wedges in the basket twice during cooking.

6 Repeat with the remaining wedges. Serve immediately.

COOKING TIP While cooking the second batch, keep the first batch of cooked sweet potatoes warm in an oven heated to 200°F.

PER SERVING Calories: 95; Fat: 3g (28% of calories from fat); Saturated Fat: 0g; Protein: 1g; Carbohydrates: 18g; Sodium: 37mg; Fiber: 2g; Sugar: 3g; 190% DV vitamin A; 3% DV vitamin C

Brown Rice Fritters

PREP 10 minutes / **COOK** 8 to 10 minutes / **SERVES** 4

380°F

Gluten-Free, Vegetarian

1 (10-ounce) bag frozen cooked brown rice, thawed

1 egg

3 tablespoons brown rice flour

⅓ cup finely grated carrots

⅓ cup minced red bell pepper

2 tablespoons minced fresh basil

3 tablespoons grated Parmesan cheese

2 teaspoons olive oil

AREN'T YOU GLAD YOU DIDN'T DEEP-FRY

Deep-fried vegetable fritters can contain as much as 55% of their calories from fat.

Fritters can be made of everything from apples to a plain batter. These fritters are made with brown rice and lots of veggies so they pack a nutritional punch. Serve them with a fresh salsa for a nice snack or a light lunch.

1 In a small bowl, combine the thawed rice, egg, and flour and mix to blend.

2 Stir in the carrots, bell pepper, basil, and Parmesan cheese.

3 Form the mixture into 8 fritters and drizzle with the olive oil.

4 Put the fritters carefully into the air fryer basket. Air-fry for 8 to 10 minutes, or until the fritters are golden brown and cooked through.

INGREDIENT TIP You can make your own brown rice for this recipe. Just put ½ cup of brown rice into a saucepan and cover with ¾ cup water. Cover and simmer for 20 to 30 minutes or until the rice is tender. Let the rice cool before you use it in this recipe.

PER SERVING Calories: 143; Fat 5g (33% calories from fat); Saturated Fat: 2g; Protein 5g; Carbohydrates: 19g; Sodium: 97 mg; Fiber 1g; Sugar: 0g; 11% DV vitamin A; 27% DV vitamin C

Cheesy Roasted Sweet Potatoes

PREP 7 minutes / **COOK** 18 to 23 minutes / **SERVES** 4

400°F

Family Favorite, Gluten-Free

2 large sweet potatoes, peeled and sliced (see Tip)

1 teaspoon olive oil

1 tablespoon white balsamic vinegar

1 teaspoon dried thyme

¼ cup grated Parmesan cheese

Sweet potatoes are really delicious when simply roasted with Parmesan cheese and herbs. Serve this side dish with a roasted chicken or a grilled steak.

1 In a large bowl, drizzle the sweet potato slices with the olive oil and toss.

2 Sprinkle with the balsamic vinegar and thyme and toss again.

3 Sprinkle the potatoes with the Parmesan cheese and toss to coat.

4 Roast the slices, in batches, in the air fryer basket for 18 to 23 minutes, tossing the sweet potato slices in the basket once during cooking, until tender.

5 Repeat with the remaining sweet potato slices. Serve immediately.

SUBSTITUTION TIP Make this recipe with Yukon Gold or russet potatoes, too. The cooking time will be a bit less. Leave the peel on the Yukon Golds or russets, if you like, for more fiber.

PER SERVING Calories: 100; Fat: 3g (27% of calories from fat); Saturated Fat: 1g; Protein: 4g; Carbohydrates: 15g; Sodium: 132mg; Fiber: 2g; Sugar: 4g; 189% DV vitamin A; 3% DV vitamin C

Tex-Mex Roasted New Potatoes

PREP 3 minutes / **COOK** 22 to 27 minutes / **SERVES** 4

370°F

Gluten-Free, Vegan

1 pound new potatoes, rinsed and patted dry

1 onion, chopped

4 garlic cloves, minced

2 jalapeño peppers, minced

2 teaspoons olive oil

2 teaspoons chili powder

½ teaspoon ground cumin

½ teaspoon dried oregano

Potatoes are the chameleons of the vegetable world. Because their flavor is so mild and mellow, they can be combined with many flavors and cuisines. The spicy Tex-Mex flavors of jalapeño peppers, onions, garlic, and chili powder wake up this simple side dish and add personality to your plate.

1 In a medium metal bowl, mix the potatoes, onion, garlic, and jalapeños.

2 Add the olive oil and toss to coat.

3 Sprinkle with the chili powder, cumin, and oregano. Toss again.

4 Place the bowl in the air fryer and roast the potatoes for 22 to 27 minutes, shaking the bowl once during cooking, until tender and slightly crispy. Serve immediately.

INGREDIENT NOTE New potatoes are "thinned out" early in the growth cycle so the rest of the crop can mature. They are the second harvest of the potato season (creamer potatoes are the first harvest). "Baby" potatoes are the next crop picked.

PER SERVING Calories: 123; Fat 3g (22% of calories from fat); Saturated Fat: 0g; Protein: 3g; Carbohydrates: 22g; Sodium: 61mg; Fiber: 3g; Sugar: 3g; 9% DV vitamin A; 34% DV vitamin C

Fried Green Tomatoes

PREP 15 minutes / **COOK** 6 to 8 minutes / **SERVES** 4

400°F

Family Favorite,
Vegetarian

4 medium green tomatoes

⅓ cup all purpose flour

2 egg whites

¼ cup almond milk

1 cup ground almonds

½ cup panko bread crumbs

2 teaspoons olive oil

1 teaspoon paprika

1 clove garlic, minced

AREN'T YOU GLAD YOU DIDN'T DEEP-FRY

A typical slice of a deep-fried Fried Green Tomato has 73% calories from fat.

Fried Green Tomatoes is a classic Southern recipe that was developed to use up tomatoes that had not ripened before the first frost. It may be difficult to find green tomatoes in the market, so look at a farmers' market, or grow them yourself! Or you can try this recipe with firm red tomatoes.

1 Rinse the tomatoes and pat dry. Cut the tomatoes into ½-inch slices, discarding the thinner ends.

2 Put the flour on a plate. In a shallow bowl, beat the egg whites with the almond milk until frothy. And on another plate, combine the almonds, bread crumbs, olive oil, paprika, and garlic and mix well.

3 Dip the tomato slices into the flour, then into the egg white mixture, then into the almond mixture to coat.

4 Place four of the coated tomato slices in the air fryer basket. Air fry for 6 to 8 minutes or until the tomato coating is crisp and golden brown. Repeat with remaining tomato slices and serve immediately.

COOKING TIP Don't crowd the tomatoes in the air fryer basket or they won't get crisp. Cook in three or four batches if you have to. You can keep the fried tomatoes warm in a 250°F oven for up to 15 minutes.

PER SERVING Calories: 105; Fat 2g (17% of calories from fat); Saturated Fat: 0g; Protein: 4g; Carbohydrates: 18g; Sodium: 57mg; Fiber: 1g; Sugar: 4g; 11% DV vitamin A; 32% DV vitamin C

Honey-Roasted Pears with Ricotta, p. 138

DESSERTS

Honey-Roasted Pears with Ricotta

PREP 7 minutes / **COOK** 18 to 23 minutes / **SERVES** 4

350°F

Gluten-Free, Vegetarian, Very Low Sodium

2 large Bosc pears, halved and seeded (see Tip)

3 tablespoons honey

1 tablespoon unsalted butter

½ teaspoon ground cinnamon

¼ cup walnuts, chopped

¼ cup part-skim low-fat ricotta cheese, divided

Roasted fruit tastes completely different than raw fruit. Roasting caramelizes the sugars in the pears here, giving them a slightly smoky-toffee flavor. For this recipe, choose firm pears that give only slightly when pressed with your fingers. Leave the peel on so the pears hold their shape as they roast. You can leave the stem on half the pears for a pretty presentation. The ricotta cheese adds creamy smoothness to the slightly crisp pears.

1 In a 6-by-2-inch pan, place the pears cut-side up.

2 In a small microwave-safe bowl, melt the honey, butter, and cinnamon. Brush this mixture over the cut sides of the pears.

3 Pour 3 tablespoons of water around the pears in the pan. Roast the pears for 18 to 23 minutes, or until tender when pierced with a fork and slightly crisp on the edges, basting once with the liquid in the pan.

4 Carefully remove the pears from the pan and place on a serving plate. Drizzle each with some liquid from the pan, sprinkle the walnuts on top, and serve with a spoonful of ricotta cheese.

SUBSTITUTION TIP Bosc pears are the best choice for this recipe because they are firm, even when ripe. You can use Anjou pears instead; they may take less time to cook.

PER SERVING Calories: 138; Fat: 4g (26% of calories from fat); Saturated Fat: 3g; Protein: 2g; Carbohydrates: 25g; Sodium: 17mg; Fiber: 3g; Sugar: 21g; 3% DV vitamin A; 5% DV vitamin C

Grilled Spiced Fruit

PREP 10 minutes / **COOK** 3 to 5 minutes / **SERVES** 4

400°F

*Fast, Gluten-Free,
No Sodium, Vegetarian*

2 peaches, peeled, pitted,
and thickly sliced

3 plums, halved and pitted

3 nectarines, halved
and pitted

1 tablespoon honey

½ teaspoon ground
cinnamon

¼ teaspoon ground allspice

Pinch cayenne pepper

Stone fruits threaded onto skewers and grilled with honey and spices make a delicious and easy dessert. You can serve these fruits over frozen yogurt or low-fat ice cream if you like. They are also delicious for breakfast with plain yogurt.

1 Thread the fruit, alternating the types, onto 8 bamboo (see Tip, page 79) or metal skewers that fit into the air fryer.

2 In a small bowl, stir together the honey, cinnamon, allspice, and cayenne. Brush the glaze onto the fruit.

3 Grill the skewers for 3 to 5 minutes, or until lightly browned and caramelized. Cool for 5 minutes and serve.

SUBSTITUTION TIP Try apples, pineapple, or even straw-berries. If you choose other fruits, pair them on skewers with fruits that cook in about the same time.

PER SERVING Calories: 121; Fat: 1g (7% calories from fat); Saturated Fat: 0g; Protein: 3g; Carbohydrates: 30g; Sodium: 0mg; Fiber: 4g; Sugar: 25g; 16% DV vitamin A; 27% DV vitamin C

Caramelized Peaches with Blueberries

PREP 10 minutes / **COOK** 7 to 11 minutes / **SERVES** 6

380°F

*Gluten-Free, Vegetarian,
Very Low Sodium*

3 peaches, peeled, halved, and pitted (see Tip)

2 tablespoons packed brown sugar

1 cup plain nonfat Greek yogurt

1 teaspoon pure vanilla extract

¼ teaspoon ground cinnamon

1 cup fresh blueberries

Fruits caramelize so beautifully in the air fryer. This process is similar to the Maillard reaction, in which compounds break down in the heat and re-form to add color and flavor to the food. Serve the warm peaches with cold yogurt and sweet blueberries.

1 Place the peaches, cut-side up, in the air fryer basket. Sprinkle evenly with the brown sugar. Bake for 7 to 11 minutes, or until they start to brown around the edges and become tender.

2 Meanwhile, in a small bowl, stir together the yogurt, vanilla, and cinnamon.

3 When the peaches are done, transfer them to a serving plate. Top with the yogurt mixture and the blueberries. Serve immediately.

PREPARATION TIP To peel peaches easily, cut a small X in the bottom of each. Place the peaches in boiling water for about 10 seconds. Remove and plunge into ice water. The peel should now easily slip off.

PER SERVING Calories: 98; Fat: 1g (10% calories from fat); Saturated Fat: 0g; Protein: 5g; Carbohydrates: 20g; Sodium: 20mg; Fiber: 4g; Sugar: 18g; 9% DV vitamin A; 16% DV vitamin C

Stuffed Apples

PREP 13 minutes / **COOK** 12 to 17 minutes / **SERVES** 4

350°F

Gluten-Free, Vegan,
Very Low Sodium

4 medium apples, rinsed and patted dry (see Tip)

2 tablespoons freshly squeezed lemon juice

¼ cup golden raisins

3 tablespoons chopped walnuts

3 tablespoons dried cranberries

2 tablespoons packed brown sugar

⅓ cup apple cider

Apples are stuffed with a mix of nuts and dried fruit and baked to tender perfection in this easy recipe. This treat evokes thoughts and smells of fall. Serve this warming dessert with low-fat yogurt or top it with softly whipped cream for a decadent treat. Of course, the apples are delicious (and healthy) all on their own, too!

1 Cut a strip of peel from the top of each apple and remove the core, being careful not to cut through the bottom of the apple. Sprinkle the cut parts of the apples with lemon juice and place in a 6-by-2-inch pan.

2 In a small bowl, stir together the raisins, walnuts, cranberries, and brown sugar. Stuff one-fourth of this mixture into each apple.

3 Pour the apple cider around the apples in the pan.

4 Bake in the air fryer for 12 to 17 minutes, or until the apples are tender when pierced with a fork. Serve immediately.

INGREDIENT TIP Choose the best apples for baking that will keep their shape. Those varieties include Granny Smith, Jonagold, McIntosh, and Cortland. Apples should be firm, free of bruises, and heavy for their size.

PER SERVING Calories: 122; Fat: 4g (29.5% of calories from fat); Saturated Fat: 0g; Protein: 1g; Carbohydrates: 22g; Sodium: 8mg; Fiber: 1g; Sugar: 20g; 5% DV vitamin C

Apple-Peach Crisp

PREP 10 minutes / **COOK** 10 to 12 minutes / **SERVES** 4

380°F

No Sodium, Vegetarian

1 apple, peeled and chopped

2 peaches, peeled, pitted, and chopped

2 tablespoons honey

½ cup quick-cooking oatmeal

⅓ cup whole-wheat pastry flour

3 tablespoons packed brown sugar

2 tablespoons unsalted butter, at room temperature

½ teaspoon ground cinnamon

This traditional fall dessert is made with a combination of cooked fruit topped with an oatmeal streusel. You can use any type of fruit, such as nectarines in place of the peaches, or pears in place of the apple. This cozy treat will conjure memories of quiet times by the fire on a crisp fall day.

1 In a 6-by-2-inch pan, thoroughly mix the apple, peaches, and honey.

2 In a medium bowl, stir together the oatmeal, pastry flour, brown sugar, butter, and cinnamon until crumbly. Sprinkle this mixture over the fruit.

3 Bake for 10 to 12 minutes, or until the fruit is bubbly and the topping is golden brown. Serve warm.

SUBSTITUTION TIP If you have a healthy granola cereal you like, use that in place of the oatmeal mixture. Sprinkle about 1 cup over the fruit and bake as directed.

PER SERVING Calories: 237; Fat: 7g (26% calories from fat); Saturated Fat: 4g; Protein: 3g; Carbohydrates: 44g; Sodium: 1mg; Fiber: 5g; Sugar: 28g; 4% DV vitamin A; 2% DV vitamin C

Strawberry-Rhubarb Crumble

PREP 10 minutes / **COOK** 12 to 17 minutes / **SERVES** 6

370°F

No Sodium, Vegetarian

1½ cups sliced fresh strawberries

¾ cup sliced rhubarb

⅓ cup sugar

⅔ cup quick-cooking oatmeal

½ cup whole-wheat pastry flour

¼ cup packed brown sugar

½ teaspoon ground cinnamon

3 tablespoons unsalted butter, melted

Strawberries and rhubarb are the fruits of spring. They are delicious combined in this dessert with a cinnamon-scented oatmeal streusel baked on top. This is wonderful served with low-fat ice cream melting into each warm bite.

1 In a 6-by-2-inch metal pan, combine the strawberries, rhubarb, and sugar.

2 In a medium bowl, mix the oatmeal, pastry flour, brown sugar, and cinnamon.

3 Stir the melted butter into the oatmeal mixture until crumbly. Sprinkle this over the fruit. Bake for 12 to 17 minutes, or until the fruit is bubbling and the topping is golden brown. Serve warm.

INGREDIENT NOTE Did you know that rhubarb is technically a vegetable? It is very tart and needs some sugar to be edible, but it is full of fiber and loaded with vitamin C.

PER SERVING Calories: 206; Fat: 7g (30% calories from fat); Saturated Fat: 4g; Protein: 3g; Carbohydrates: 36g; Sodium: 1mg; Fiber: 4g; Sugar: 21g; 4% DV vitamin A; 42% DV vitamin C

Mixed Berry Crumble

PREP 10 minutes / **COOK** 11 to 16 minutes / **SERVES** 4

380°F

Family Favorite, No Sodium, Vegetarian

½ cup chopped fresh strawberries

½ cup fresh blueberries

⅓ cup frozen raspberries

1 tablespoon freshly squeezed lemon juice

1 tablespoon honey

⅔ cup whole-wheat pastry flour (see Tip)

3 tablespoons packed brown sugar

2 tablespoons unsalted butter, melted

A crumble is simply fruit topped with a sweetened streusel mixture and baked until the fruit is tender and bubbly and the topping is browned. It makes a satisfying simple dessert or a great contribution to a potluck. Use any type of berries you like in this recipe—whether just one type or a mix of your favorites. Whole-wheat pastry flour is between all-purpose flour and whole-wheat flour, having more nutrients and fiber than plain white flour. You can find it in some large grocery stores and online.

1 In a 6-by-2-inch pan, combine the strawberries, blueberries, and raspberries. Drizzle with the lemon juice and honey.

2 In a small bowl, mix the pastry flour and brown sugar.

3 Stir in the butter and mix until crumbly. Sprinkle this mixture over the fruit.

4 Bake for 11 to 16 minutes, or until the fruit is tender and bubbly and the topping is golden brown. Serve warm.

INGREDIENT TIP If you can't find whole-wheat pastry flour, use a mix of half whole-wheat flour and half all-purpose flour as a substitute.

PER SERVING Calories: 199; Fat: 6g (27% of calories from fat); Saturated Fat: 4g; Protein: 3g; Carbohydrates: 35g; Sodium: 1mg; Fiber: 4g; Sugar: 17g; 4% DV vitamin A; 27% DV vitamin C

Apple-Blueberry Hand Pies

PREP 20 minutes / **COOK** 7 to 9 minutes / **SERVES** 4

400°F

Vegetarian, Very Low Sodium

1 medium Granny Smith apple, peeled and finely chopped

½ cup dried blueberries

1 tablespoon freshly squeezed orange juice

1 tablespoon packed brown sugar

2 teaspoons cornstarch

4 sheets frozen phyllo dough, thawed

8 teaspoons unsalted butter, melted

8 teaspoons sugar

Nonstick cooking spray, for coating the phyllo dough

AREN'T YOU GLAD YOU DIDN'T DEEP-FRY

Give yourself a hand for losing almost half the calories from fat.

Hand pies are small packets of fruit-filled phyllo dough. Recipes made with phyllo are usually layered with butter to create the characteristic flaky layers, but here we'll use cooking spray to reduce the fat content.

1 In a medium bowl, mix the apple, blueberries, orange juice, brown sugar, and cornstarch.

2 Place 1 sheet of phyllo dough on a work surface with the narrow side facing you. Brush very lightly with 1 teaspoon of butter and sprinkle with 1 teaspoon of sugar. Fold the phyllo sheet in half from left to right.

3 Place one-fourth of the fruit filling at the bottom of the sheet in the center. Fold the left side of the sheet over the filling. Spray lightly with cooking spray. Fold the right side of the sheet over the filling. Brush with 1 teaspoon of butter and sprinkle with 1 teaspoon of sugar.

4 Fold the bottom right corner of the dough up to meet the left side of the pastry sheet to form a triangle. Continue folding the triangles over to enclose the filling, as you would fold a flag. Seal the edge with a bit of water. Spray lightly with cooking spray. Repeat with the remaining 3 sheets of the phyllo, butter, sugar, and cooking spray, making four pies.

5 Place the pies in the air fryer basket. Bake for 7 to 9 minutes, or until golden brown and crisp. Remove the pies and let cool on a wire rack before serving.

SUBSTITUTION TIP   This recipe is also wonderful with chopped peaches and dried cherries, or use dried cherries in place of the blueberries with the apples.

PER SERVING Calories: 239; Fat: 8g (30% calories from fat); Saturated Fat: 5g; Protein 2g; Carbohydrates: 42g; Sodium: 34mg; Fiber: 5g; Sugar: 23g; 9% DV vitamin A; 8% DV vitamin C

Oatmeal-Carrot Cookie Cups

PREP 10 minutes / **COOK** 8 to 10 minutes / **MAKES** 16 cups

350°F

Gluten-Free

3 tablespoons unsalted butter, at room temperature

¼ cup packed brown sugar

1 tablespoon honey

1 egg white

½ teaspoon vanilla extract

⅓ cup finely grated carrot (see Tip)

½ cup quick-cooking oatmeal

⅓ cup whole-wheat pastry flour

½ teaspoon baking soda

¼ cup dried cherries

Cookie cups are a combination of a cake and cookie, baked in muffin cups. Oatmeal and grated carrot add nutritional value to these little gems, and dried cherries add texture and flavor. If you like, top each with a drizzle of caramel ice cream sauce before serving.

1 In a medium bowl, beat the butter, brown sugar, and honey until well combined.

2 Add the egg white, vanilla, and carrot. Beat to combine.

3 Stir in the oatmeal, pastry flour, and baking soda.

4 Stir in the dried cherries.

5 Double up 32 mini muffin foil cups to make 16 cups. Fill each with about 4 teaspoons of dough. Bake the cookie cups, 8 at a time, for 8 to 10 minutes, or until light golden brown and just set. Serve warm.

SUBSTITUTION TIP Try substituting a grated apple for the carrot in your next batch. Or throw caution to the wind and add some grated chocolate instead!

PER SERVING (1 cookie cup) Calories: 127; Fat: 5g (35% calories from fat); Saturated Fat: 3g; Protein: 2g; Carbohydrates: 20g; Sodium: 88mg; Fiber: 1g; Sugar: 12g; 7% DV vitamin A

Dark Chocolate Oatmeal Cookies

PREP 10 minutes / **COOK** 8 to 13 minutes / **MAKES** 30 cookies

320°F

Vegetarian,
Very Low Sodium

3 tablespoons
unsalted butter

2 ounces dark chocolate,
chopped (see Tip)

½ cup packed brown sugar

2 egg whites

1 teaspoon pure
vanilla extract

1 cup quick-cooking
oatmeal

½ cup whole-wheat
pastry flour

½ teaspoon baking soda

¼ cup dried cranberries

These chewy, rich, and really delicious cookies are packed with oatmeal, whole-wheat pastry flour, and dark chocolate. Dried cranberries add a tart note. And they are good for you! Enjoy one with a cup of coffee for a morning break or tuck some in a lunch box for a sweet surprise.

1 In a medium metal bowl, mix the butter and dark chocolate. Bake in the air fryer for 1 to 3 minutes, or until the butter and chocolate melt. Stir until smooth.

2 Beat in the brown sugar, egg whites, and vanilla until smooth.

3 Stir in the oatmeal, pastry flour, and baking soda.

4 Stir in the cranberries. Form the dough into about 30 (1-inch) balls. Bake the dough balls, in batches of 8, in the air fryer basket for 7 to 10 minutes, or until set.

5 Carefully remove the cookies from the air fryer and cool on a wire rack. Repeat with the remaining dough balls.

INGREDIENT TIP Dark chocolate is good for your heart! Chocolate that is at least 70 percent cocoa solids is the type to choose. It contains flavonoids that help repair cell damage and may reduce blood pressure, improve blood flow to the heart, and prevent blood clots. So enjoy—in moderation, of course.

PER SERVING (1 cookie) Calories: 55; Fat: 2g (33% of calories from fat); Saturated Fat: 1g; Protein: 1g; Carbohydrates: 8g; Sodium: 25mg; Fiber: 1g; Sugar: 4g; 1% DV vitamin A

Pumpkin Pie Pudding

PREP 10 minutes / **COOK** 12 to 17 minutes / **SERVES** 4

350°F

Vegetarian

Nonstick cooking spray, for coating the pan

1 cup canned no-salt-added pumpkin purée (not pumpkin pie filling)

¼ cup packed brown sugar

3 tablespoons all-purpose flour

1 tablespoon unsalted butter, melted

1 egg

2 tablespoons 1 percent milk

1 teaspoon pure vanilla extract

4 low-fat vanilla wafers, crumbled

Pumpkin pie is a relatively healthy dessert that is full of vitamin A. But the crust adds tons of fat, so let's make a pudding instead—for the same flavor and texture—and crumble a few low-fat vanilla wafers on top to mimic a crust.

1 Spray a 6-by-2-inch pan with nonstick cooking spray and set aside.

2 In a medium bowl, whisk the pumpkin, brown sugar, flour, butter, egg, milk, and vanilla until combined. Pour the pumpkin mixture into the prepared pan.

3 Bake for 12 to 17 minutes, or until the pudding is set and registers 165°F on a thermometer.

4 Remove the pudding from the air fryer and cool on a wire rack.

5 To serve, scoop the pudding into bowls and top with vanilla wafer crumbs.

SERVING TIP If you're feeling decadent, serve this pudding warm with frozen yogurt or ice milk on top.

PER SERVING Calories: 154; Fat: 5g (29% calories from fat); Saturated Fat: 3g; Protein: 3g; Carbohydrates: 26g; Sodium: 39mg; Fiber: 2g; Sugar: 16g; 194% DV vitamin A; 4% DV vitamin C

Appendix A
AIR FRYER COOKING CHART

This is a general chart for reference. Your air fryer may have different cooking times and temperatures. Follow the instructions that came with your appliance. Always cook foods, especially meats, poultry, and seafood, until done to a safe internal temperature.

CATEGORY	INGREDIENT	QUANTITY	TEMP	TIME	NOTES
Breads	Muffins	10 muffins	360°F	10 to 12 minutes	Place the muffins inside double foil cups; place in a single layer in the air fryer.
Fruit	All types	2 to 4 cups	320°F	Soft fruits: 3 to 5 minutes Hard fruits: 5 to 10 minutes	Cook hard fruits, such as apples, and soft fruits, such as peaches, together. Cook hard fruits in some liquid in a pan.
Vegetables	Asparagus	1 pound	380°F	4 to 8 minutes	Snap off tough ends before cooking.
	Bell peppers	1 to 2 cups	370°F	5 to 8 minutes	Cut into 1-inch strips.
	Broccoli florets	2 to 4 cups	390°F	5 to 8 minutes	Lightly spray with oil; sprinkle with salt and freshly ground black pepper.
	Carrots	1 to 2 cups	370°F	6 to 10 minutes	Slice ¼ inch thick.
	Cauliflower florets	2 to 4 cups	390°F	5 to 9 minutes	Mist with oil and season before frying. Shake once during cooking.

CATEGORY	INGREDIENT	QUANTITY	TEMP	TIME	NOTES
Vegetables (continued)	French fries, thick, fresh	2 to 4 cups	400°F	15 to 25 minutes	Lightly spray with oil.
	French fries, thick, frozen	2 to 4 cups	380°F	12 to 20 minutes	If there is any ice on the fries, remove it.
	French fries, thin, fresh	2 to 4 cups	400°F	15 to 20 minutes	Pat dry; toss with cornstarch and ½ teaspoon sugar for better browning; mist with oil; toss once during cooking.
	French fries, thin, frozen	2 to 4 cups	390°F	10 to 14 minutes	If there is any ice clinging to the fries, remove it; toss once during cooking.
	Mushrooms	1 to 2 cups	380°F	6 to 9 minutes	Trim stems before cooking.
	Potatoes, chopped	4 to 7 cups	400°F	13 to 19 minutes	Spray with oil; toss once or twice during cooking.
	Potatoes, sliced	4 to 5 cups	380°F	10 to 15 minutes	Slice about ⅛ inch thick; toss with oil; toss during cooking.
	Potato wedges	2 to 4 cups	390°F	18 to 22 minutes	Lightly spray with oil; sprinkle with salt and freshly ground black pepper.
	Sweet potato cubes (1 inch)	4 to 6 cups	390°F	14 to 20 minutes	Lightly spray with oil.
Vegetables, root	All except potatoes and sweet potatoes	2 to 4 cups	400°F	15 to 25 minutes	Peel and cut into 1-inch chunks.
Vegetables, tender	Eggplant, sliced	1 to 3 pounds	350°F	15 to 20 minutes	Toss halfway through cooking.
	Green beans, whole	1 to 3 pounds	350°F	5 to 7 minutes	Shake halfway through cooking.
	Onion	1 to 3 pounds	350°F	4 to 7 minutes	Sliced onions work better than chopped; cut into similar sizes. Shake halfway through cooking.

CATEGORY	INGREDIENT	QUANTITY	TEMP	TIME	NOTES
Vegetables, tender *(continued)*	Tomatoes, whole	1 to 3 pounds	350°F	8 minutes	Shake halfway through cooking.
	Tomatoes, sliced			4 minutes	
	Tomatoes	3 to 4 cups	350°F	7 to 12 minutes	Halve and remove the seeds.
	Zucchini	1 to 3 pounds	350°F	10 minutes	Shake halfway through cooking.
Fish and Shellfish	Fish fingers, frozen	1 to 3 cups	390°F	8 to 10 minutes	If any ice is clinging to the fish, remove it.
	Salmon fillets	4 (6-ounce) fillets	300°F	9 to 14 minutes	Brush with oil and sprinkle with seasonings; cook to 140°F.
	Salmon steak	4 (8-ounce) steaks	300°F	14 to 18 minutes	Brush with oil and sprinkle with seasonings; cook to 140°F.
	Shrimp, fresh	1 to 2 pounds	390°F	5 minutes	Shell and devein shrimp; pat dry. Bread before cooking, if desired.
	Shrimp, frozen			8 minutes	
Poultry	Chicken breast	1 to 6 (6-ounce) boneless skinless breast halves	360°F	10 to 16 minutes	Place in a single layer in the air fryer basket; turn once during cooking.
	Chicken drumsticks	1 to 6 drumsticks	400°F and 320°F	8 minutes at 400°F; 10 to 12 minutes at 320°F	Pat dry; do NOT rinse. Spray with oil and sprinkle with seasonings.
	Chicken nuggets, frozen	1 to 4 cups	370°F	7 to 12 minutes	If any ice is clinging to the chicken, remove it.
	Chicken wings	1 to 3 pounds	380°F	15 to 20 minutes	Cook to 165°F; toss once during cooking.
Pork	Chops	1 to 4 (1-inch-thick) chops	350°F	7 to 10 minutes	Cook to at least 145°F. Place in a single layer; turn once during cooking.
	Tenderloin	1 pound	400°F	9 to 11 minutes	Cut into ½-inch slices.

CATEGORY	INGREDIENT	QUANTITY	TEMP	TIME	NOTES
Meat	Burgers	1 to 4 (4-ounce) patties	360°F	6 to 9 minutes	Place in a single layer; turn once during cooking. Cook to 160°F.
	Meatballs, fresh (raw)	25 per batch	390°F	6 to 9 minutes	Don't crowd the cooker; place in a single layer in the basket; turn with tongs halfway through cooking.
	Meatballs, frozen	25 per batch	380°F	6 to 8 minutes	If any ice is clinging to the meatballs, remove it.
	Steak	1 to 4 (6-ounce) steaks, ¾ inch thick	360°F	8 to 12 minutes	Time depends on desired doneness; use a meat thermometer to cook to 140°F for medium-rare or to 160°F for well done.
Other	Egg rolls	6 to 8	390°F	3 to 6 minutes	Brush or spray with oil before cooking.
	Pizza	1 pizza	390°F	5 to 10 minutes	Place the pizza on parchment in the basket. Make sure it fits into the basket.

Appendix B
DIRTY DOZEN AND CLEAN FIFTEEN

A nonprofit and environmental watchdog organization called Environmental Working Group (EWG) looks at data supplied by the US Department of Agriculture (USDA) and the Food and Drug Administration (FDA) about pesticide residues and compiles a list each year of the best and worst pesticide loads found in commercial crops. You can refer to the Dirty Dozen list to know which fruits and vegetables you should always buy organic. The Clean Fifteen list lets you know which produce is considered safe enough when grown conventionally to allow you to skip the organics. This does not mean that the Clean Fifteen produce is pesticide-free, though, so wash these fruits and vegetables thoroughly.

These lists change every year, so make sure you look up the most recent before you fill your shopping cart. You'll find the most recent lists as well as a guide to pesticides in produce at EWG.org/FoodNews.

2017 DIRTY DOZEN		2017 CLEAN FIFTEEN	
Apples	Strawberries	Asparagus	Kiwis
Celery	Sweet bell peppers	Avocados	Mangoes
Cherries	Tomatoes	Cabbage	Onions
Grapes	*In addition to the Dirty Dozen, the EWG added a food contaminated with highly toxic organo-phosphate insecticides:*	Cantaloupe	Papayas
Nectarines		Cauliflower	Pineapples
Peaches		Eggplant	Sweet corn
Pears		Grapefruit	Sweet peas (frozen)
Potatoes	Hot peppers	Honeydew melon	
Spinach			

Appendix C
CONVERSION TABLES

VOLUME EQUIVALENTS (DRY)

US STANDARD	METRIC (APPROXIMATE)
⅛ teaspoon	0.5 mL
¼ teaspoon	1 mL
½ teaspoon	2 mL
¾ teaspoon	4 mL
1 teaspoon	5 mL
1 tablespoon	15 mL
¼ cup	59 mL
⅓ cup	79 mL
½ cup	118 mL
⅔ cup	156 mL
¾ cup	177 mL
1 cup	235 mL
2 cups or 1 pint	475 mL
3 cups	700 mL
4 cups or 1 quart	1 L
½ gallon	2 L
1 gallon	4 L

VOLUME EQUIVALENTS (LIQUID)

US STANDARD	US STANDARD (OUNCES)	METRIC (APPROXIMATE)
2 tablespoons	1 fl. oz.	30 mL
¼ cup	2 fl. oz.	60 mL
½ cup	4 fl. oz.	120 mL
1 cup	8 fl. oz.	240 mL
1½ cups	12 fl. oz.	355 mL
2 cups or 1 pint	16 fl. oz.	475 mL
4 cups or 1 quart	32 fl. oz.	1 L
1 gallon	128 fl. oz.	4 L

OVEN TEMPERATURES

FAHRENHEIT (F)	CELSIUS (C) (APPROXIMATE)
250°F	120°C
300°F	150°C
325°F	165°C
350°F	180°C
375°F	190°C
400°F	200°C
425°F	220°C
450°F	230°C

Appendix D
RESOURCES

General Knowledge

These references will help you increase your knowledge about heart health and general nutrition. The nutrition sites provide a lot of information about the benefits of healthy foods.

American Heart Association
Learn how to protect your heart through diet, exercise, and medical care: www.heart.org/HEARTORG.

American Heart Association Healthy Eating Guidelines
These are the general guidelines I used to develop the recipes in this book: www.heart.org/HEARTORG/HealthyLiving/HealthyEating/Healthy-Eating
_UCM_001188_SubHomePage.jsp.

Livestrong.com
Learn more about healthy eating and how to choose the best foods for your body: www.livestrong.com/cat/food-and-drink.

The World's Healthiest Foods
Find nutrition information for just about every food in the world at this site: www.whfoods.com.

Air Fryer Manuals

Most manuals for air fryers can be downloaded from the Web. It can be helpful to download these for more ideas, recipes, and tips.

Digital Air Fryer
Manual includes tips on maintenance and troubleshooting as well as a cooking chart: www.belliniappliances.com/electrical/documents/BTDF950_U&C_140730a.pdf.

GLiP Oil-less Air Fryer
Instruction manual includes a helpful chart for cooking meats, potatoes, and snacks: http://cache.air-n-water.com/manuals/glip-af800white-manual.pdf.

GoWISE USA Air Fryer
Instruction manual contains instructions for cleaning, troubleshooting, and a cooking guide: http://airfryerchips.com/wp-content/uploads/2015/10/GW22621_AirFryer_Manual.pdf.

Philips HD9220/20
A user manual, quick start guide, and recipe booklet are all available online: www.p4c.philips.com/cgi-bin/cpindex.pl?ctn=HD9220/20&scy=GB&slg=ENG.

Todd English Air Fryer
Manual includes easy recipes: https://sva.ccnsite.com/gallery/24204853/Todd-English-Air-Fryer-Manual.

Websites with Recipes

Some websites have delicious and easy recipes for the air fryer.

Airfry.blogspot.com
Interesting and unusual vegetarian Indian recipes for the air fryer, including veggie fingers, falafel, and cheese spinach balls.

Australian Allrecipes
http://allrecipes.com.au/recipes/tag-8775/air-fryer.aspx
A couple dozen of their top-rated, viewer-reviewed air fryer recipes, including crumbed chicken tenderloins, chocolate cake in an air fryer, and schnitzel parmigiana.

Hotairfrying.com
Maintained by Philips Air Fryers. This site includes ideas for using the air fryer in new ways, along with recipes for foods such as crispy jalapeño poppers, air-fried tomatoes, and green curry noodles.

Powerairfryer.com
www.powerairfryer.com/recipes.php
Great recipes, including blooming onion, coconut shrimp, and roasted chicken with herbs.

Recipethis.com
https://recipethis.com/tag/airfryer-recipes/
Fun recipes for this appliance, such as paleo pumpkin muffins, fruit crumble mug cakes, and vegetable fries.

Serving Sizes

American Heart Association
To learn more about what a true "serving" is, visit www.heart.org/HEARTORG /Caregiver/Replenish/WhatisaServing/What-is-a-Serving_UCM_301838 _Article.jsp.

RECIPE INDEX

	PAGE	FAMILY FAVORITE	FAST	GLUTEN-FREE	NO SODIUM	VEGAN	VEGETARIAN	VERY LOW SODIUM
Apple Pork Tenderloin	110			X				
Apple-Blueberry Hand Pies	145						X	X
Apple-Peach Crisp	142				X		X	
Asian Swordfish	80			X				
Asparagus and Bell Pepper Strata	27						X	
Asparagus with Garlic	128		X	X		X		
Avocado and Egg Burrito	26	X	X				X	
Barbecued Chicken	98	X		X				
Beans and Greens Pizza	50						X	
Beef and Broccoli	119	X		X				
Beef and Fruit Stir-Fry	120			X				
Beef Risotto	121			X				
Broccoli-Spinach Dip	61			X			X	
Brown Rice and Beef-Stuffed Bell Peppers	118			X				
Brown Rice Fritters	132			X			X	
Buffalo Cauliflower Snacks	67	X		X			X	
Buttermilk Fried Chicken	99	X						
California Melts	42		X				X	
Caramelized Peaches with Blueberries	140			X			X	X
Carrot and Cinnamon Muffins	30						X	
Cheesy Roasted Sweet Potatoes	133	X		X				
Chicken Croquettes	52							
Chicken Fajitas	97	X						

	PAGE	FAMILY FAVORITE	FAST	GLUTEN-FREE	NO SODIUM	VEGAN	VEGETARIAN	VERY LOW SODIUM
Chicken and Fruit Bruschetta	53							
Chicken Sausages	28			X				X
Chicken with 20 Cloves of Garlic	100			X				
Cinnamon-Pear Chips	59			X	X	X		
Cranberry Turkey Quesadillas	103	X	X					
Cran-Bran Muffins	31	X					X	
Crispy Broccoli	125			X		X		
Crispy Mustard Pork Tenderloin	109							
Crispy Sweet Potato Wedges	131	X		X		X		
Crustless Veggie Quiche	48			X			X	
Curried Brussels Sprouts	127			X		X		X
Curried Chicken with Fruit	94			X				
Dark Chocolate Oatmeal Cookies	147						X	X
Dried Fruit Beignets	32						X	X
Espresso-Grilled Pork Tenderloin	111			X				
Falafel	44					X		X
Fish and Vegetable Tacos	75	X						
French Toast Sticks with Strawberry Sauce	34	X	X				X	
Fried Green Tomatoes	135	X					X	
Garlic-Roasted Bell Peppers	126			X		X		X
Glazed Carrots and Sweet Potatoes	129			X			X	
Glazed Chicken Wings	168	X		X				
Greek Chicken Kebabs	92			X				
Greek Vegetable Skillet	116			X				
Grilled Cheese and Greens Sandwiches	40						X	
Grilled Chicken Mini Pizzas	51	X						
Grilled Spiced Fruit	139		X	X	X		X	
Hearty Greens Chips with Curried Yogurt Sauce	60			X			X	
Herbed-Roasted Vegetables	124			X		X		X
Honey-Roasted Pears with Ricotta	138			X			X	X
Kale Chips with Tex-Mex Dip	56		X	X			X	

	PAGE	FAMILY FAVORITE	FAST	GLUTEN-FREE	NO SODIUM	VEGAN	VEGETARIAN	VERY LOW SODIUM
Lemon-Garlic Chicken	101			X				
Light Herbed Meatballs	117							
Lighter Fish and Chips	76	X						
Loaded Mini Potatoes	47	X					X	X
Mini Chicken Meatballs	69	X						
Mini Turkey Meatloaves	102	X		X				
Mixed Berry Crumble	144	X			X		X	
Mustard-Crusted Fish Fillets	74		X					
Nutty Chicken Nuggets	90	X						
Oatmeal-Carrot Cookie Cups	146			X				
Phyllo Vegetable Triangles	63	X					X	
Pork Burgers with Red Cabbage Salad	108	X						
Pork and Fruit Kebabs	113			X				
Pork and Mixed Greens Salad	106			X				
Pork and Potatoes	112	X		X				
Pork Satay	107			X				
Pumpkin Donut Holes	29						X	X
Pumpkin Pie Pudding	148						X	
Purple Potato Chips with Chipotle Sauce and Rosemary	58			X			X	
Ratatouille	38					X		X
Roasted Grape Dip	62			X			X	X
Roasted Mushrooms with Garlic	65			X		X		X
Roasted Vegetable Chicken Salad	88			X				
Salmon on Bed of Fennel and Carro	82			X				
Salmon and Brown Rice Frittata	25			X				
Salmon Nachos	71			X				
Salmon Spring Rolls	81			X				
Scalloped Mixed Vegetables	130			X			X	
Scallops with Green Vegetables	84			X				
Scrambled Eggs with Broccoli and Spinach	49			X				
Snapper with Fruit	77			X				

	PAGE	FAMILY FAVORITE	FAST	GLUTEN-FREE	NO SODIUM	VEGAN	VEGETARIAN	VERY LOW SODIUM
Southwest Stuffed Mushrooms	66						X	X
Spicy Chicken Meatballs	91	X		X				
Spicy Grilled Steak	115		X	X				
Spicy Sweet Potato Fries	57	X		X			X	
Steak and Vegetable Kebabs	114	X		X				
Stir-Fried Chicken with Mixed Fruit	95			X				
Strawberry-Rhubarb Crumble	143				X		X	
Stuffed Apples	141			X		X		X
Stuffed Portobello Mushrooms	45						X	
Stuffed Tomatoes	46			X			X	
Tandoori Chicken	93	X		X				
Tex-Mex Chicken Stir-Fry	96			X				
Tex-Mex Roasted New Potatoes	134			X		X		
Tex-Mex Salmon Stir-Fry	83			X				
Three-Berry Dutch Pancake	33						X	
Tuna and Fruit Kebabs	79			X				
Tuna Wraps	78		X					
Vegetable Egg Rolls	39						X	
Vegetable Pita Sandwiches	43						X	X
Vegetable Pot Stickers	64					X		
Vegetable Shrimp Toast	70							
Veggie Frittata	24			X			X	
Veggie Tuna Melts	41	X						
Warm Chicken and Spinach Salad	89			X				

INDEX